BOARD
GAMES

o o o

BOARD GAMES

The Changing Shape of Corporate Power

∘ ∘ ∘

**ARTHUR FLEISCHER, JR.,
GEOFFREY C. HAZARD, JR.,
MIRIAM Z. KLIPPER**

LITTLE, BROWN AND COMPANY
BOSTON   TORONTO   LONDON

FIRST EDITION

Library of Congress Cataloging-in-Publication Data

Fleischer, Arthur, 1933–
Board games.

1. Consolidation and merger of corporations—
United States—Case studies.   I. Hazard, Geoffrey C.
II. Klipper, Miriam Z.   III. Title.
HD2746.5.F64   1988   338.8'3'0973   88-9471

10 9 8 7 6 5 4 3 2 1

FG

Published simultaneously in Canada
by Little, Brown & Company (Canada) Limited

PRINTED IN THE UNITED STATES OF AMERICA

To Nathaniel and Alexander,
and in memory of Bill Cary and Sam Harris,
each a master of the corporate law.

◦   ◦   ◦

Contents

o o o

Acknowledgments

We are grateful to many people whose help we deeply appreciate in the writing of this book.

We thank Roger Donald and Rick Tetzeli, our editors at Little, Brown; Stuart Z. Katz, Morris Mendelson, Judith Platt, Judith Higgins, and Peter D. Danforth for perceptive editorial comments; Myles Slatin for a masterful critique; and Julius Groebel, Jr., for long-remembered instruction. Peter Shepherd, our literary agent, generously gave much of his time and thought to our project.

We also thank Warren Gordon, Susanne Fordham, Donna Marie Osborne, Joann Bradley, Renee Penner, Barbara Albrecht, and Sylvia Siegle, as well as Fried, Frank, Harris, Shriver & Jacobson's word processing staff, whose support made the completion of this book possible within the present merger era.

BOARD
GAMES

• • •

o o o

The Parsley on the Fish

I RVING OLDS, chairman of U.S. Steel in the "good old days" of 1940 to 1952, is quoted as saying: "Directors are merely the parsley on the fish." Many collected their checks and accepted with grace and a good deal of pleasure a new appliance each year, top of the line.

This may once have been true, but no more. Megamergers, hostile takeovers, leveraged buyouts, and corporate restructurings have radically transformed the directors' role in the power structure of the American corporation. This transformation has evolved in the financial and legal dynamics of several struggles for control of major U.S. corporations. In the competition for control of our corporations, the boardroom is where the battles are fought and concluded.

The revolution in the directors' role has to be put in perspective. It is a big ripple on top of an economic wave, on top of an oceanic change in the world economy. Until two decades or so ago, American corporations were masters of their destinies, or thought they were; American business had a virtual monopoly on the American market — half of the world economy at the time — and dominated markets everywhere else. Remember? American oil companies, also known as the Seven Sisters, controlled the world market in petroleum. General Motors dominated automobiles, RCA reigned supreme in radio and TV, and Xerox meant copier. Our steel industry — led by U.S. Steel, the product of J. P. Morgan's great merger, and over which Irving Olds had presided — produced half the world's steel and more than half of the high-quality, high-profit lines.

In the 1960s, however, American business corporations began to face competition they had not encountered since 1914. The Japanese invasion of the automobile market is a classic illustration. For years, General Motors and the other members of the Big Three, Ford and Chrysler, said that nobody wanted to buy those small automobiles, and besides that, the Japanese made lousy cars. The American car makers began to notice in the 1960s that in Marin County, California, 50 percent of the sales were of Japanese cars, but they thought that was because everyone there lived in hot tubs. The U.S. auto elite did not realize this was the advance party. By the time they did, the Japanese were so far down the road that it has taken ten years for the United States to get back in the race, and it may take them forever to catch up.

On top of the oceanic flood of economic change have been waves of change in corporate finance. Managers of major American companies in the post–World War II period from 1945 to 1965 also enjoyed substantial control over their own capital resources. Since corporate taxation hit profits heavily and dividends still more heavily, a corporation could multiply its effective payout to shareholders by plowing earnings back into its own operations instead of recording them as profits and paying dividends. The corporate strategy was to have a healthy balance sheet — little debt and a surplus of cash. In fact, many American corporations practically controlled everything but their costs, and those they could pass on to consumers.

In many companies, a difficult policy question faced by the directors was setting executive compensation: pay, bonuses, pension rights, and stock options. Legally and economically, executive compensation involves a conflict of interest because the executive is dealing with the company he manages. Executive-compensation matters coming before the board of directors therefore involved carefully developed legal procedures, as they still do. They also could involve embarrassment stemming from the fact that the CEO's salary was fixed by the board, while the makeup of the board at that time was generally fixed by the CEO. Often, the CEO along with other inside directors also constituted the majority. But if the board overcame that embarrassment, as it typically could, it was parsley all the way.

Today's corporate managers and directors operate in a changed environment and therefore experience their roles differently. Management performance is being judged by world competitive standards. Most large American business corporations directly confront, in their own backyards, competition from businesses in every other part of the world — businesses that are run by relentless competitors who have their own sources of manpower, innovation, and capital, and often the overt or covert support of their governments.

Even business competition within the United States has become far more dynamic as a result of greater technical innovation and product change, to mention only two factors. Hence, every business is much more vulnerable than in the past to the adverse consequences of ineffective management. An investor can no longer invest in a "good sound company" and simply relax. That good sound company might turn out to be Republic Steel or Swift & Company. Neither can management assume that they "have it made" when they have "made it." "We have to earn our wings every day," as Frank Borman, then CEO of Eastern Airlines, said before he lost his.

Fifty years ago "portfolio theory" was unknown by that name and was embryonic in content: "You should have an oil, some steel and good municipals. . . ." Today's shareholders want returns and have hired professional investors to measure whether the returns are adequate. The pattern of stock ownership and control has changed so much that an increasing portion is held by institutional investors. Indeed, more than 50 percent of the outstanding shares of the Fortune 500 companies is held by institutional investors with professional portfolio managers. Elaborate calculations can now be made — and are being made — of risk and return on a virtually infinite array of hypothetical portfolios.

Portfolio managers focus on short-run returns, partly out of simple technological feasibility. It is now possible to make precise, rapid comparison of present returns and discounted future returns on investment alternatives where before it was technically impossible. This means that the theory and practice of stock ownership itself have changed. Whether the emphasis on short-run returns is inappropriate or not is another question.

Still another overall change has been the declining significance of the antitrust laws. Many potential mergers of yesteryear, friendly or unfriendly, foundered on antitrust concerns. These days antitrust obstacles are infrequently raised, partly as a result of change in government policy, which of course is subject to further change. More fundamental, however, is change in the theoretical underpinnings of antitrust policy, in which the doctrine that "bigness is badness" no longer is generally accepted by people who understand the subject. Still more fundamental is the fact that the antitrust laws by definition are concerned with competition in the "relevant market." Until as recently as ten years ago, the relevant market in a particular product or service usually was defined in terms of American companies competing in the American market. Now the relevant market in certain industries must take into account the rest of the world. By that standard even IBM does not dominate "the market."

With these changes — a world market, an altered pattern of stock ownership, and a more promising government antitrust policy — almost no company in the early 1980s, whatever its size, remained safe from a hostile takeover. Another key factor at work was the increased real value of existing corporate assets. In 1986, prices paid by raiders on the initial bid were more than twenty times the after-tax earnings of the targets. Raiders were paying top dollar.

Takeovers involve an attempt by an outsider to reorganize

a viable corporate enterprise, without management's approval, through some kind of a buyout. To defend, directors may restructure the corporation to provide greater value to shareholders. The board of directors' responsibility continues until a takeover is consummated or defeated. The takeover is a high-speed, high-stakes drama enacted by players with now-familiar sobriquets — *raiders, target management, outside directors, white knights, investment bankers.* It has standard props: *crown jewels, junk bonds, poison pills, LBOs.* And a takeover, like the attack on Pearl Harbor, is "no drill."

When the takeover movement started in the 1970s, it was stimulated by inflation, then running 10 percent per year and higher. Assets as reported on corporate balance sheets were undervalued. Raiders bought companies by borrowing, calculating that they would pay back with cheaper dollars. Although a buyer might have to borrow at 12 or 15 percent, with inflation running at 15 percent the effective interest rate could be 5 percent or less. The buyer repaid the loan with depreciated dollars, while the acquired assets appreciated.

In the eighties, inflation and interest rates both sharply declined. But there were still situations where corporate assets were worth more to a raider than was reflected in the stock market. One component of this differential is the "premium for control." The stock market is a retail market for a hundred shares, a thousand shares, five thousand shares, not a wholesale market for millions of shares in which control as such is bought and sold. It is exceedingly difficult to buy control in the market. What can be bought in the stock market is enough shares to launch a proxy contest or achieve close to a blocking position: a level of stock ownership, in the neighborhood of 20 to 25 percent, that may inhibit others from seeking to acquire control of the company and that will enable the holder to influence the business and management of the company.

Normally, stock ownership is so dispersed that the "voters" cannot get together behind a slate of directors to oppose the management slate. Or else stock is held by investors — often institutions — who rarely vote against a management slate. A

raider, however, can acquire enough shares to create, so to
speak, his own rival party. In practice, he does not have to
buy a majority of a company's stock in order to compel incumbent management to recognize his demands as to how
the company will be managed. The threat to disrupt the in-
cumbents' control is enough. (After all, Mayor Richard Daley
didn't have to control all the votes in Chicago — just enough
to keep the Republicans from trying to bother him.)

The premium for control is the extra value in the shares
held in this position. The raider may have to pay for this premium value when, for example, after buying ten thousand
shares to establish a concentrated position, his buying is likely
to push up the share price because there is more demand for
the shares relative to the supply.

Obtaining control, and having to pay a premium to get it,
are not worthwhile unless the raider thinks he can do something that present management is not doing. Otherwise, the
company would be worth no more in the raider's hands. There
may be any number of ways a raider thinks he can get more
out of the company. Essentially, all of them boil down to running the existing business more efficiently — "cutting out the
fat" — or reconfiguring the business so that it does better in
its markets — "improving the fit" — or realizing the value in
one or more lines of the target's business that are not reflected in the market — "busting up the target."

Cutting the fat, improving the fit, and busting up the target
responded to the economic situation of the 1980s. The end of
inflation was accompanied by a rise in the real rate of interest.
This in turn raised the cost of new capital, correspondingly
increased the real value of existing corporate assets, and de-
creased the relative attractiveness of equity holdings compared with fixed-income securities. Corporate assets of existing companies could be bought relatively cheaply if strategies
could be found to get greater yield from them.

The stock market puts a value on the stock of the company
as a whole and in so doing does not value the different pieces.
Thus, in arriving at the stock price of a conglomerate with

diverse businesses, the market does not differentiate between the Widget Division and the Level Division. A shrewd buyer could know that the Widget Division is a high-multiple growth structure and that the Level Division is a stable cash producer — a cash cow. If he bought the conglomerate, he could sell off the Widget Division at a big premium and get the Level Division as a bargain. Therefore, even after the raider paid the premium for control, he would have a cushion left and could acquire the leftover business for little or nothing.

The forces that have brought about a more competitive market in the control of companies are also responsible for the radically altered role of the director. The very survival of a corporation now depends on the board of directors' abilities to deal effectively — within the new boundaries of law and regulation — with acquisitions, takeovers, and defenses against takeovers.

The strategies of takeover offense and defense have both become more aggressive. As raiders develop new techniques, the boards of target corporations have had to counter with new defenses to maximize shareholder values. Companies that build up large internal capital resources, not reflected in the price of the stock, virtually invite a takeover. Boards therefore now begin restructuring before raiders make their company a target. They try to capture the underlying asset values for their shareholders rather than let the raider have them. From the viewpoint of the target company, the best defense is a "fully" priced stock.

Other defenses include various "shark repellents," such as staggered boards and "fair price" provisions and "poison pills"; certain of these defenses require shareholder approval, while the poison pill can be adopted by the directors alone. In formulating its defensive tactics, the corporation's board now has broad power to determine whether and how a corporation will exist and, if it survives, how it will be restructured. Directors now exercise in fact powers that they previously held only formally.

Back when directors were parsley, Adolph Berle and Gardiner Means could write in their classic work, *The Modern Corporation and Private Property,* "In still larger view, the modern corporation may be regarded not simply as one form of social organization but potentially (if not yet actually) as the dominant institution of the modern world." Berle and Means also asserted that effective control of the modern corporation had shifted away from the stockholders: "The property owner who invests in a modern corporation so far surrenders his wealth to those in control of the corporation that he . . . may become merely the recipient of the wages of capital."

In fact, the shift in power that Berle and Means had noticed ran from the stockholders *and* the directors *to* professional management, i.e., the full-time paid employee officers of the corporation, particularly the CEO. This was the point made by Irving Olds, who was, after all, just such a CEO.

Berle and Means also called attention to the fact that "physical control over the instruments of production" had passed from the individual owners to the management of these large corporations. *Physical* control of the "instruments of production" is not necessarily irrelevant, as revealed by the sit-down strike, the lockout, and expropriation of industry by revolutionary governments, all of which involve change of physical control. But physical control of instruments of production is practically irrelevant under normal peaceful conditions. Kings of old did not get rich by keeping their hands on the plows or the bellows. Under a viable system of law and government, possession is not nine points of the law or even more than one or two points. The serious question is, What is the control over those who have physical control of the instruments of production?

The short answer is that greater control of the corporation's instruments of production has come to be exercised by the board. Moreover, within the last decade the composition of the board of directors has shifted. When Berle and Means wrote, many boards had few directors unaffiliated with the company. Often, indeed, a majority or a substantial part of the board consisted of inside management directors. In the 1980s the reverse is true. Looking at the Fortune 500 companies, it is clear that employee directors are a minority; outside, independent directors are dominant, and the change is clearly a continuing trend. Independent directors first achieved supremacy in number, and now they have achieved supremacy in power.

The powers and legal responsibilities of corporate directors and officers derive from corporate law. To be secure, power has to be legitimate, and for power to be legitimate, whether public or private, it has to be accountable. The modern business corporation is accountable according to its constitutional law, just as the government is accountable according to constitutional law. The constitutional law of the business corporation is called the law of corporate governance, which defines the accountability of directors to shareholders and of officers to directors. Corporate-governance law is important law because ultimately it affects every shareholder and the entire economy.

Corporate-governance law attracted wide concern during the 1970s, when public opinion was aroused by disclosure of dramatic violations of law by corporate officials who seemed to defy accountability to their shareholders and even to their own directors. The corporate-governance problems of the seventies were business variations on Watergate: ITT's ventures in Chile; Lockheed's payment of bribes in Japan; and Gulf Oil's illegal political contributions. As a result of these and other scandals, legal controls on corporations were tightened. The tightening of these controls partially resolved the corporate-governance problem of the 1970s.

The corporate-governance problem of the 1980s and 1990s is not corporate corruption but corporate competence, which is of vastly greater importance in terms of the country's material well-being. The corporation's ability to function as a competitive enterprise, and thus its economic competence, can be directly affected by its constitutional structure.

A comparison can be made with the structure of government. Corruption in government captures headlines and damages the fabric of society. But structural weakness in the government — for example, in the functioning of Congress — can affect the country even more adversely. Corporate-governance law likewise directly affects the competence of American business corporations: competence in the international competitive market; competence of top management within business corporations; competence of the board in seeing that management meets the standard that world competition requires.

The law of corporate governance is governed by state rather than federal law. To a large extent it is decisional law made by judges rather than statutory law made by legislatures. Although the language of the statutes on which corporation law is based is old and general, in the last decade decisional law has been crucial in more specifically defining director responsibility. Hence, the private "constitutional" law for corporations has been worked out in the decisions of judges passing upon specific situations — takeover attempt by takeover attempt, case by case.

The problem of American corporate competence thus has taken on a peculiar legalistic character, like almost everything else in this country's political culture. As de Tocqueville said in *Democracy in America* in 1835: "There is hardly a political question in the United States which does not sooner or later turn into a judicial one. . . . In the United States the lawyers constitute power which . . . enwraps the whole of society."

Since the large-scale business enterprise is the central institution of the modern world economy, the directors of these corporations have come to have responsibilities that affect everyone's welfare. There is, therefore, a connection between the responsibility of the directors of corporations and the distress of American industry in today's world economy. But it is essential to keep the causal connection straight. John Kenneth Galbraith, writing about the stock market disaster of 1929, said: "The stock market is but a mirror which . . . provides an image of the underlying or *fundamental* economic situation. Cause and effect run from the economy to the stock market, never the reverse."

Similarly, the boardroom is a mirror of fundamental change in business. "Cause and effect" generally run from the economy to the boardroom, not the reverse. Change in the economic environment of present-day American business has expanded the nature of director responsibility.

The changes both in the economic environment and the role of directors appear most vividly in corporate takeovers. A takeover or threatened takeover compresses the history and prospects of a company into a month and crystallizes all that a business venture might be into a mere number — the bottom line of the last offer. Takeovers are vivid illustrations of changed business conditions and responsibilities. The leading-edge law they have created has vitally altered the shape of corporate power.

∘ ∘ ∘

Nine Honorable Men

FOR THE DIRECTORS of the corporations that dominate or influence the lives of most U.S. citizens, January 29, 1985, was a black day. It was the day the Supreme Court of Delaware found several of Chicago's best and brightest business leaders guilty of breaching their duty to the company's shareholders. Nine directors of the billion-dollar blue-chip Trans Union Corporation were held liable for agreeing to sell the company without careful review of its value and ordered personally to pay the difference between the per share selling price and the "real" market value of the company's shares.

A motion by the directors for a rehearing summed up the crisis: The court's decision "has shocked the corporate world in its unprecedented holding that knowledgeable directors of a Delaware corporation, performing their statutory managerial function, may be exposed to catastrophic liability . . . where there were no charges or proof of fraud, bad faith or self-dealing."

Jerome Van Gorkom, sixty-three, chairman of the board of Trans Union and its chief executive officer for more than seventeen years, was the man who made the deal. He was a lawyer and a CPA and knew all about acquisition procedures and how to value a company. Van Gorkom was also a director of Illinois-based IC Industries, Inc., three other large corporations, and the popular Lyric Opera of Chicago. In 1979, Chicago bankers had recommended him for a City of Chicago review board on the basis of "his highly respected business and finance abilities."

Other key company officers on the Trans Union board, in the words of Delaware Supreme Court Judge Henry R. Horsey, wore "their badge of expertise in the corporate affairs of Trans Union on their sleeves."

Most of Trans Union's independent directors — outside directors who were not employees of the corporation — had been on its board for a decade or more. With the exception of W. Allen Wallis, all were chief executive officers of major Chicago-based corporations. Wallis was a renowned mathematical economist who had been a professor at Yale University, dean of the Graduate Business School at the University of Chicago, and chancellor of the University of Rochester. At the time of the Trans Union negotiations, he was a director of Bausch and Lomb, Kodak, Metropolitan Life Insurance Company, Standard Oil, and other corporations. In 1982, he became U.S. under secretary of state for economic affairs.

William B. Johnson, a director since 1969, was chairman and chief executive officer of IC Industries, Inc., a $3.7 billion diversified holding company.

Joseph B. Lanterman was retired chairman of Amsted Industries and also a director of International Harvester, Harris Trust and Savings Bank, Peoples Energy Corporation, Illinois Bell Telephone Company, and Kemper Insurance Company.

Graham J. Morgan was chairman and chief executive officer of U.S. Gypsum, a $1.5 billion building-materials and industrial-products manufacturer. He had been involved in more than thirty corporate takeovers.

Robert Reneker had been president and chief executive officer of Swift & Company and was a board member of seven other corporations, including the Chicago Tribune Company.

These eminent men were held personally liable to Trans Union's shareholders for $23.5 million.

In 1980, Trans Union was thriving as a major transportation, manufacturing, and financial services conglomerate with sales totaling $1.1 billion. Incorporated under the laws of Delaware, Trans Union operated through forty-nine subsidiaries, including Union Tank Car Company, which manufactured and leased the world's second-largest fleet of privately owned railway tank cars. Trans Union's other businesses included leasing ships and trucks, processing sulfur, manufacturing mining equipment, and supplying systems for water- and waste-treatment systems.

Members of Trans Union's board received regular, detailed financial reports and five-year operating and earnings projections. The company was profitable. However, it did not generate enough taxable income to absorb all the tax credits resulting from purchases of new equipment. To stimulate investment in machinery and equipment, the tax laws permitted purchasers of heavy capital equipment to claim an income tax credit (ITC) for every purchase. Trans Union had steadily accumulated large unused ITCs.

Along with other capital-intensive companies, Trans Union had lobbied Congress to allow companies that could not make full use of ITCs to cash them in for tax refunds. During the summer of 1980, Van Gorkom had testified before congressional committees in this effort. By the end of August, however, he realized the lobbying effort would fail.

Trans Union's 1980 annual revised five-year forecast projected that there would be a healthy annual income growth of about 20 percent and that the company would have about $195 million in spare cash, "with surplus [cash] growing rapidly from 1982 onward." Four alternative uses of the projected cash surplus were proposed: buy back stock to increase earnings per share; increase dividends; launch a major acquisition program; or some combination of these possibilities. The report emphasized that "we have sufficient time to fully develop our course of action."

In an August meeting between Van Gorkom and his senior managers, another alternative was suggested — selling Trans Union to a company with large taxable income, which could make use of Trans Union's tax credits. Donald Romans, executive vice president and chief financial officer of Trans Union, made an alternative proposal — a leveraged buyout (LBO) by an investor group that would include incumbent management. It would buy the company from Trans Union's public shareholders and take it private, to be run by the Trans Union management.

In an LBO, the equity investor group as a rule puts up only a small percentage of the purchase price; the major portion of the price is financed with borrowed funds secured by the company's assets. The transaction involves a prediction that the company's cash flow can repay the debt within five to ten years. For a stable company with sufficient cash flow, the investor group usually can offer a price well above market for the publicly held shares. After most of the debt is repaid, the company can be resold to the public or to another company, possibly with big profits for the original buyout group.

Romans testified at trial that his department had done a "preliminary study" of a leveraged buyout — a "rough cut at seeing whether a cash flow would support what might be considered a high price for this type of transaction."* According to Romans, the analysis was not aimed at establishing a fair price per share of the stock but was to determine the cash flow needed to pay interest and principal on the debt that would "probably" be incurred in a leveraged buyout, without "any benefit of experts to identify what the limits were." He and his staff merely "ran the numbers" at $50 and $60 a share with the "rough form" of their cash figures at the time, which "indicated that $50 would be very easy to do but $60 would be very difficult to do."

Van Gorkom, who owned almost 61,000 shares, plus options to purchase more than 15,000 shares at $34 per share, said that he would take $55 per share for his own shares. However, after a staff meeting on September 5, 1980, he ve-

---

*Throughout the manuscript, quotes with no reference indicated are from the decision of the court in the case under discussion. See "Notes," p. 219.

toed a leveraged buyout on the grounds that it would involve an improper conflict of interest.

o   o   o

For several days following the September 5 meeting, Van Gorkom considered selling the company and thought about whether Trans Union should approach a privately held or public company as a potential buyer. Van Gorkom decided to approach Jay A. Pritzker, a close friend and skiing companion. Jay Pritzker was chairman of the board of Chicago-based Marmon Group, Inc., a unit of the Pritzker private holding company. In June 1970, Marmon, run by Jay's brother Robert A. Pritzker, had sales of just over $100 million; ten years later its sales from diversified businesses totaled $1.9 billion. The Pritzker family was also the principal shareholder in the Hyatt hotel chain.

J. Ira Harris, then of Salomon Brothers' Chicago offices, summed it up, as reported by the *New York Times*: "Wall Street recognizes Jay Pritzker as one of the nation's foremost deal makers. Jay Pritzker has a unique ability to look at a situation, analyze it very quickly and understand it thoroughly. . . . Jay never gets carried away."

Van Gorkom had consulted none of Trans Union's board members and none of its senior management except Trans Union's controller, Carl Peterson. Van Gorkom warned Peterson not to let anyone know what he was doing and, without telling Peterson why, directed him to calculate the feasibility of a leveraged buyout at $55 per share, which was roughly twice book value of the company. At $55 per share, Van Gorkom estimated, the company was worth $690 million. Van Gorkom told Peterson to use that figure and to assume a $200 million equity contribution by the buyer. Based on these assumptions, Peterson was to determine whether the $490 million debt portion of the purchase price could be paid off by the company within five years. Peterson set to work.

Van Gorkom had in mind that the debt could be repaid through the company's cash flow, as projected in the most recent five-year forecast, and by the sale of certain weaker divisions identified in a study of Trans Union by the Boston Consulting Group, an international management consulting firm. Peterson reported that at the end of five years, $50 million to $80 million of the purchase price would remain outstanding; hence, the company could not repay the debt in five years at $55 per share. Van Gorkom was disappointed but decided to meet with Pritzker anyway.

On Saturday, September 13, Van Gorkom and Pritzker met at Pritzker's home. Van Gorkom went beyond exploring Pritzker's interest in acquiring Trans Union. He had in hand a proposed per share price for the company and a financing structure to effect the sale. Van Gorkom testified that he said, "I can, I think, show how you can pay a substantial premium over the present stock price and pay off most of the loan in the first five years. . . . If you could pay $55 [per share] for this company, here is a way in which I think it can be financed." Pritzker mentioned $50 as a more attractive figure, but no other price was mentioned.

Van Gorkom then said that to verify $55 per share as the best possible price, Trans Union should be free to accept any better offer. Pritzker agreed — on one condition: that the Marmon Group would serve as a "stalking horse" for an "auction contest" if it could first acquire 1,750,000 shares of Trans Union treasury stock at market price, then in the range of $35–$37 per share.

The following Monday, Pritzker suggested a merger at $55 in cash for each Trans Union share. On Tuesday and Wednesday Pritzker met privately with Van Gorkom; Trans Union's controller, Peterson; its president and chief operating officer, Bruce S. Chelberg; and a representative from the Boston Consulting Group. "[I was] astounded," Van Gorkom said, "that events [were] moving with such amazing rapidity." On Thursday Pritzker offered $55 per share, subject to first buying 1 million shares of Trans Union treasury stock (7.4 percent) at $38 per share. And Pritzker insisted that the Trans Union board act on the proposal within three days.

The following day, Friday, September 19, Van Gorkom, Chelberg, and Pritzker consulted Trans Union's lead bank to form a syndicate to finance the transaction. On the same day, Van Gorkom retained James Brennan as outside counsel to advise Trans Union on the merger. Pritzker's lawyer was to draft the merger documents. The documents were reviewed by Van Gorkom's lawyer, in Pritzker's words, "sometimes with discussion and sometimes not, in the haste to get [the deal] finished." Van Gorkom did not consult William Browder, a company director and senior vice president and former head of Trans Union's legal department. Nor did he consult the company's legal staff or other senior management. He scheduled a Trans Union board meeting for the next day, Saturday, September 20, at noon, and a meeting of senior management for an hour before that.

Of the senior management present on September 20, only Chelberg and Peterson knew about Pritzker's offer. Van Gorkom described the offer to the other members of management but did not provide copies of the proposed merger agreement. Romans reported a revised study of a leveraged buyout, showing a feasible price range of $55 to $65 per share. Van Gorkom did not look at the study and did not ask Romans to make it available for the board meeting.

Only Chelberg and Peterson supported the Pritzker proposal. The other members of senior management, hearing it for the first time, were completely negative. Romans, it was later testified, thought the price too low "in relation to what [Trans Union] could derive for the company in a cash sale, particularly one which enabled us to realize the values of certain subsidiaries and independent entities."

Romans was also concerned that an all-cash deal would require shareholders who had bought low to pay capital gains taxes. He also objected that selling the treasury stock to Pritzker and prohibiting active solicitation of other bids amounted to a "lock up"; it was an "agreed merger as opposed to an offer."

The board meeting was held as scheduled. All directors were

present except Thomas O'Boyle, who was hospitalized. Romans attended, but Van Gorkom had not invited Salomon Brothers, the company's investment banker. In a twenty-minute opening, Van Gorkom reviewed Trans Union's ITC status and his discussions with Pritzker. Van Gorkom did not inform the board of how he had arrived at the $55 figure or of the fact that it was he who proposed that price to Pritzker. Copies of the proposed merger agreement were delivered to the directors — but without time for study before or during the meeting.

The deal was:

- Pritzker would pay $55 in cash for all publicly held shares of Trans Union's stock. Trans Union would be merged into New T Company, which would be a wholly owned subsidiary of the GL Corporation, the Pritzker private holding company.
- Pritzker had the right to buy 1 million newly issued Trans Union shares at $38 per share.
- For a ninety-day period, Trans Union could receive competing offers but not actively solicit them.
- Trans Union could furnish to competing bidders only published information and not proprietary information.
- The offer was subject to Pritzker's obtaining the necessary financing by October 10, 1980. If financing was not committed to by 5:00 P.M. of that day, the deal was off.
- The offer had to be acted on by the board by the next evening.

Van Gorkom said that putting Trans Union "up for auction" through a ninety-day market test would verify $55 as a fair price. In his words, the "free market will have an opportunity to judge whether $55 was . . . fair." Van Gorkom did not ask the board's opinion of whether $55 per share was the best obtainable price. He asked whether the $55 price was a fair enough price that Trans Union stockholders should be given the opportunity to accept or reject. "Whether to let the stockholders decide it [is] all you are being asked to decide today," he said.

Romans told the board that his studies were not a valuation of the company stock but a projection of the feasibility of a leveraged buyout. The study "ran the numbers at 50 and 60 and then the subsequent study at 55 and 65," he said, "and that [is] not the same thing as saying that I have a valuation of the company at X dollars. But it [is] . . . a first step towards reaching that conclusion." In his opinion, $55 was "in the range of a fair price, [but] at the beginning of the range."

Chelberg supported Van Gorkom in "the necessity to act immediately on this offer" and about "the adequacy of the $55 and the question of how that would be tested." James Brennan, outside counsel, advised the board that they might be sued if they failed to accept the offer. He also advised that an outside valuation opinion was not legally required.

After a meeting of about two hours, the board approved the proposed agreement. Later they claimed to have attached two conditions: that Trans Union could accept, though not solicit, any better offer made during a "market test" period; and that the company could share proprietary company information, as well as published information, with potential bidders other than the Pritzkers.

That evening, in the midst of a formal party he was hosting for the opening of the Lyric Opera of Chicago, Van Gorkom executed the agreement. The court later found that "neither he nor any other director read the agreement prior to its signing."

o   o   o

The Trans Union press release issued September 22 announced a "definitive" merger agreement between Trans Union and the Marmon Group: "The merger is subject to approval by the stockholders of Trans Union at a special meeting expected to be held sometime during December or early January." The release made no reference to Trans Union's being available at a higher offer or being allowed to withdraw from the agreement before the forthcoming shareholder meeting. News of Marmon's bid sent the price of Trans Union's stock up 14½ points to $51.50 per share.

As reported in the *New York Times* the following day, "The Pritzkers have always had a good sense of value," one analyst noted. "Trans Union produces a large, stable cash flow. Its assets are long-lived, have a low obsolescence factor and are therefore undervalued. Marmon is picking up a very solid company."

News of the merger created a revolt in the ranks of Trans Union's management. Jack Kruizenga, head of the tank car operations — Trans Union's most profitable division — informed Van Gorkom that fifteen key officers would resign unless the merger was called off. Said Van Gorkom at a later deposition: "Kruizenga was very angry. He was angry at me personally, and the reason is he felt that he and his group had been very successful in building up the rail car leasing — which is perfectly true — and he felt that we should not have sold the company. . . . He had had no reward in the stock price, but he felt that if they kept doing as well as they had been doing, that eventually the market would realize the value and would raise the market price, . . . and I said, 'Jack, the record gives no reason for assuming that that will happen. Our earnings have doubled in the last ten years and our stock is selling exactly where it was ten years ago, for all practical purposes.' . . .

"But, in essence, his reason was that he and his people wanted to remain in a public company so that they could continue to operate as they had with the eventual hope that the stock of Trans Union would rise without being bought by somebody. And that is a perfectly legitimate attitude but quite different from that of Mr. [Sidney H.] Bonser [executive vice president of Trans Union] and Mr. Romans who, frankly, as I eventually learned, thought that a leveraged buyout would eventually put the two of them in the two top offices in the company. Quite different motives."

Q: — Mr. Kruizenga's position was that given time the market would realize that the stock was undervalued?

A: — Yes.

Q: — And that was different from your opinion?

A: — I can't say what is going to happen in the future. I can only say that based on the past, if I thought that, I wouldn't have sold the company, either.

The threatened resignations triggered a new round of private discussions between Van Gorkom and Pritzker. Pritzker suggested that the agreement be amended to permit Trans Union to solicit, as well as receive, higher offers, and that the shareholders' meeting be postponed from early January to February 10 to allow more time for offers before a shareholder vote. The quid pro quo was that the dissidents agree to remain with the company for at least six months after the merger.

The plan worked, at least in the short run. On October 8, at Van Gorkom's invitation, the board met to amend the merger agreement to give Trans Union the unfettered "right to openly solicit offers through January 31." The company's investment banker, Salomon Brothers, was authorized to seek offers during the proposed market test period. Neither Van Gorkom nor any other board member then or later asked the investment banking firm for a fairness opinion of Pritzker's proposal or for a valuation of Trans Union as an entity. At the October 8 meeting, however, the directors approved the proposed amendments to the agreement with Pritzker, sight unseen.

But the next day, "Pritzker moved swiftly to off-set the effect of the amendments." He announced completion of financing arrangements for the acquisition, thereby binding Trans Union to an unconditional agreement. He also exercised his option on the treasury stock at $38; on October 9, the company's stock closed at $53.13. These facts were disclosed in a press release issued the same day.

The formal written amendments to the September 20 merger agreement still had not been prepared by Pritzker and delivered to Van Gorkom, and were delivered only on the next day, October 10. The written version was markedly different from the one Van Gorkom had presented to the board on October 8. As written, the amendments authorized Trans Union actively to seek competing offers, but it could supersede the Pritzker merger only if it obtained a firm offer at a higher price before February 10, 1981, the date of the stockholders' meeting scheduled to approve Pritzker's proposal. However, since Pritzker had already exercised his option to buy the company's shares, a buyer would confront Pritzker as the largest single stockholder, and one who would directly profit from any higher offer.

Van Gorkom, as the court found, signed all the amendments without determining whether they were "consistent with the authority previously granted him by the Board." Moreover, "the record does not affirmatively establish that Trans Union's directors ever read the October 10 amendments . . . or that any of them, including Van Gorkom, understood the opposite result of their intended effect — until it was too late."

The only offer subsequently received was a proposal by Romans and other senior Trans Union officers to take the company private. They sought help from the four-year-old investment banking firm of Kohlberg, Kravis, Roberts & Company (KKR). Romans and the KKR group — which included the Reichmann brothers, the Canadian real estate magnates — had begun discussions shortly after announcement of the proposed merger to discuss the possibility of a leveraged buyout by all members of management except Van Gorkom. By early October, Henry Kravis gave Romans written notice of KKR's "interest in making an offer to purchase 100 percent" of Trans Union's common stock. With Van Gorkom's knowledge and grudging consent, Romans's group worked with KKR to put together a proposal.

Van Gorkom explained his concern about the leveraged buyout when later questioned under oath: "It is, according to KKR, essential that the management make a substantial investment, substantial in relation to their wealth, and this gives . . . the management a larger percentage of the new company than they could possibly have in Trans Union Corporation. And as a result, it . . . gives them a vested interest in seeing that that transaction takes place, in contrast to other buyers who might be on the scene. And that is . . . a conflict of interest."

On December 2, Kravis and Romans delivered to Van Gorkom a formal offer to purchase Trans Union's assets for cash equivalent to $60 per share, contingent upon financing, which Kravis indicated was 80 percent complete. Referring to negotiations with major banks for the loan portion of the buyout, the letter stated that KKR was "confident that commitments for the bank financing . . . can be obtained within two or three weeks." Kravis advised that they were willing to enter into a "definitive agreement" under terms and conditions "substantially the same" as those in Trans Union's agreement with Pritzker. The letter, addressed to Trans Union's board, requested a meeting that afternoon.

Van Gorkom objected that the financing condition meant the proposal was not a firm offer, ignoring the fact that Pritzker's offer had been similarly conditioned. Van Gorkom refused Kravis's request to issue a press release announcing KKR's offer on the grounds that it might "chill" any other offer. Despite Van Gorkom's cool reception, Romans and Kravis left with the understanding that the KKR proposal would be presented to Trans Union's board that afternoon.

Shortly before the scheduled board meeting, however, Kravis withdrew his offer. The withdrawal was in response to a sudden decision by Jack Kruizenga — Trans Union's key operating officer, to whom Van Gorkom had spoken directly after meeting with Romans and Kravis — to back out of the KKR purchasing group. Van Gorkom admitted that he and Kruizenga had discussed Kruizenga's participation in the KKR proposal but denied responsibility for Kruizenga's change of mind. At the board meeting later that afternoon, the KKR proposal was not raised. Van Gorkom considered it "dead."

Less than three weeks later, on December 19, Burks Alden Smith filed a class action suit in the Delaware Chancery Court against Trans Union, eight of Trans Union's ten directors, the Marmon Group, the GL Corporation, New T Company, and Jay Pritzker and Robert Pritzker. Smith, founder of Smith and Loveless, Inc., a manufacturer of waste-water treatment systems that had been purchased by Trans Union more than twenty years before, owned 54,000 shares of Trans Union stock as a result of that merger. Smith sought to enjoin the Pritzker transaction, as well as damages, costs, and attorneys' fees.

On January 20, Van Gorkom attempted unsuccessfully to reopen negotiations with KKR.

In the meantime, Salomon Brothers had been searching for better offers. It sent a brochure describing Trans Union to a list of more than a hundred companies thought to be suitable merger partners. Only four showed interest: General Electric Credit Corporation (an equipment-leasing subsidiary of the General Electric Company), Borg-Warner, Bendix, and Genstar, Ltd. The only serious candidate was General Electric Credit Corporation. The evidence later showed that, had there been time, GE was prepared to offer "between $2 and $5 per share" above Pritzker's $55 per share price. However, Pritzker refused to defer the scheduled closing, and Trans Union declined to rescind its agreement with Pritzker. On January 21, GE quit. On that day, Trans Union's shareholders were sent a notice of a special meeting of stockholders on February 10.

At a lengthy meeting on January 26, the Trans Union board became more fully apprised of the events leading to the Pritzker merger agreement:

• that before September 20, only Bruce Chelberg and Carl Peterson from senior management knew that Van Gorkom had discussed a possible merger with Pritzker;

• that the $55 per share price had been suggested initially by Van Gorkom;

• that the board had not sought an independent fairness opinion;

• that at the senior management meeting on September 20, Romans and several other senior managers raised the question of the inadequacy of the $55 per share price.

On direct examination at trial, William Johnson, one of the five outside directors, was asked: "What was discussed at that [January 26] meeting?" He replied: "Everything relevant to this transaction . . . since the proxy statement of the 19th [January] had been mailed . . . General Electric had advised that they weren't going to make a bid. It was concluded to suggest that the shareholders be advised of that, and that required a supplemental proxy statement, and that required authorization of the board, and that led to a total review from beginning to end of every aspect of the whole transaction and all relevant developments . . . we went back from the beginning."

The directors voted to proceed with the Pritzker merger. The minutes of the meeting state that it was "unanimously voted that the Board of Directors continue to recommend that the stockholders vote in favor of the proposed merger, each Director being individually polled with respect to his vote." "This time we had a unanimous board," said Johnson, "where one man was missing before — to recommend the Pritzker deal. Indeed, at that point there was no other deal. And, in truth, there never had been any other deal."

On February 3, Chancellor William Marvell of the Delaware trial court denied Smith's motion to enjoin the merger. This determination did not finally decide the case; it decided only that the then-available evidence was insufficient to justify an injunction. However, denial of the injunction cleared the way for a stockholder vote.

At the scheduled shareholders' meeting a week later, the merger was approved, 69.9 percent in favor, including the nearly 8 percent stake held by Pritzker; 7.25 percent against; and 22.85 percent not voting. A few hours later, Trans Union was merged into New T Company, the wholly owned subsidiary of the Pritzker's GL Corporation, converting each share of Trans Union into a right to receive $55 per share in cash. The following day William Prickett of Prickett, Jones, Elliott, Kristol & Schnee, Smith's attorney, said he would seek to rescind the merger. "Be advised," he told the press, "the last round is not over even though the first round is." Smith, he cautioned, could seek a full trial and, if necessary, carry his fight to the Delaware Supreme Court. "I warn the Pritzkers that we will seek damages . . . and we will seek to undo this merger."

The trial took place seven months later, from September 22 through October 2, 1981. Five days after the conclusion of the trial, but before the court reached a decision, the parties stipulated to the dismissal of defendants Jay Pritzker and his brother Robert on the grounds that there was insufficient evidence against them.

On July 6, 1982, the trial court granted judgment for the directors. Its conclusion was based on two findings: first, that the board of directors had acted in an informed manner so as to have protection of the business judgment rule in approving the merger; and, second, that the shareholder vote approving the merger should not be set aside, because the stockholders had been "fairly informed." Trans Union's shareholders appealed.

o   o   o

The Delaware Supreme Court reached decision two and a half years later, in January 1985. Justice Henry Horsey, writing for a majority consisting of himself, Chief Justice Daniel Herrmann, and Justice Andrew Moore II, reversed the lower court, finding that the directors of Trans Union had not adequately informed themselves about Van Gorkom's "role in forcing the sale of Trans Union" and in accepting the value of $55 per share, and that they had failed to disclose all material information to the shareholders. The court did not decide whether $55 per share was an inadequate price.

The Trans Union directors were held liable for failure to inform themselves whether Van Gorkom did a competent job in evaluating the price and negotiating the terms of the agreement and for failing to understand the transaction. In the legal phrase, they were not "reasonably informed." They did not ask Van Gorkom: "What are the details of the agreement?" "How did you establish that it was a fair price?" Their shortcoming lay not in the decision as such, but in the inadequacy of the basis on which they made it.

As a fiduciary, a director represents the financial interests of the stockholders and has an affirmative duty to protect them.

To carry out that duty, according to Delaware law, he must "act in an informed and deliberate manner" before submitting a merger proposal to the stockholders.

The majority of the court found that the nine directors* were not informed about the intrinsic value of the company. At the first board meeting concerning the Pritzker proposal, on September 20, they had no documentation of the proposed merger, no written summary of its terms, and nothing to support the $55 per share price. The directors had relied entirely on Van Gorkom's understanding of an agreement that he had never read and that no other member of the board had ever seen.

Romans's analysis was irrelevant because it was not a valuation study, and even so, no director had recognized the significance of Romans's opinion that the $55 per share was at the "beginning of the range" of a fair price. Had the board inquired, presumably Romans would have revealed that he and senior management believed "the timing of the offer was wrong and the offer inadequate."

In light of these facts, a majority of the court found the directors "grossly negligent" in approving the transaction upon two hours' deliberation.

The directors' key defense was the "substantial" premium in Pritzker's $55 offer over Trans Union's market price of $38 per share. "The merger price offered to the stockholders . . . represented a premium of 62 percent over the average of the high and low prices at which Trans Union had traded in 1980, a premium of 48 percent over the last closing price, and a premium of 39 percent over the highest price at which the stock . . . had traded at any time during the prior six years."

They offered several other defenses as well. First, the market test period provided opportunity for other offers. Second, the board's collective experience was adequate to determine the reasonableness of the Pritzker offer. Third, their attorney,

---

*Robert Reneker had died in the course of the litigation.

Brennan, advised them that they might be sued if they rejected Pritzker's proposal. Lastly, there was the stockholders' overwhelming vote approving the merger.

The court rejected all these contentions. The premium over market price was not determinative because "in the absence of other sound valuation information, the fact of a premium alone cannot provide an adequate basis upon which to assess the fairness of an offering price." In the court's view, the market price of a publicly traded stock does not necessarily reflect the acquisition value of the company or the value of controlling the company.

As for the directors' business experience, the court noted that none of them was an investment banker or financial analyst, nor had they explored Romans's analysis, nor had they invited Salomon Brothers to assess the Pritzker offer. The court allowed that a "fairness" opinion by an independent investment banker was not essential and that reliance could be placed on valuation reports by management. But Trans Union had neither. Moreover, Van Gorkom and other directors knew that, because Trans Union was unable to use its investment for tax credits, the market had consistently undervalued the company's stock. The January 19, 1981, proxy statement stated: "In the view of the Board of Directors . . . the prices at which the Company's common stock has traded in recent years have not reflected the inherent value of the Company." In the trial court, a financial analyst testified on behalf of the shareholders that the company was worth $65 to $70 a share in a merger.

Nor did the subsequent market test validate the $55 price, because there was no real market test. The merger agreement denied the board full freedom to "shop" Trans Union or put it up for auction. The September 22 press release stated that Trans Union had entered into a "definitive agreement" with the Pritzkers, implying that the company was not at liberty to accept higher offers.

The directors relied on the action taken at the October 8 board meeting. The primary purpose of that meeting was to amend the merger agreement so that Trans Union could shop the company. At the meeting, Van Gorkom represented that Trans Union would have "an unfettered right to openly solicit offers down through January 31st." Amendments supposedly to this effect were approved. However, approval had been given without actually reviewing the amendments. In the court's view, the amendments in fact locked Trans Union into the Pritzker agreement. According to the court, the directors' conduct on October 8 simply "mirrored the deficiencies of their conduct on September 20th."

As for the effect of shareholder approval, the proxy statements for the meeting not only failed to inform the stockholders of the board's lack of valuation information but through "artful drafting cloaked this absence of information and created the mistaken impression that the board knew the intrinsic worth of the company." Because of this "absence of information," shareholder approval of the merger was not fully informed and therefore was ineffective as a ratification.

John J. McNeilly, one of the two dissenting justices, thought that "the majority opinion reads like an advocate's closing address to a hostile jury." Interpreting the facts very differently, he concluded that the Trans Union board had adequately informed itself and therefore was protected by the business judgment rule. Lawsuits and the common law itself turn on such differing interpretations. It is said that hard cases make bad law, and that is sometimes true. Certainly close cases can make hard law, as in Trans Union.

∘ ∘ ∘

The business judgment rule protects a director who acts in good faith, who is adequately informed, and who has no personal interest in the transaction. In such circumstances a director is not liable for consequences of his decision unless the decision lacks any rational basis. The rule is known as a "safe harbor," providing a director broad discretion to act without fear of judicial second-guessing. Why wasn't that harbor available to Van Gorkom and the rest of Trans Union's board?

Under corporation law as it used to work, the director's duty of due care generally amounted to a duty not to be obviously foolish. At one time directors might indeed simply have been parsley on the fish. Whatever was true before the Trans Union case, however, was not true afterward. Nine eminent directors were found to have breached their duty of care, notwithstanding the business judgment rule. Did that mean that hitherto protected business judgments would now be reviewed by judges?

"Lest we forget," said Justice McNeilly in dissent, "the corporate world . . . operates on what is so aptly referred to as 'the fast track.' These men were at the time an integral part of that world, all professional businessmen, not intellectual figureheads." Moreover, as the majority implicitly recognized, on the merits the board's decision might have been right. Van Gorkom and the board for years had been staring at Trans Union's strategic business problem, particularly the accumulated investment tax credits. Every director could have testified that he knew the business and could state why, in his independent judgment, a sale at over $50 was a good deal for the stockholders. If that is true, the directors of Trans Union made a valid business judgment. However, they apparently got bad advice as to how to document it.

Two strikingly different realities can operate when a business transaction is being put together: the reality perceived by business people and the reality perceived by lawyers. The business people are living in real time, plagued by uncertainties that often must be resolved immediately. They must decide one way or the other, on the basis of reasoning they haven't time to expound and sources of information they may not be able to sort out. The business person's focus is the bottom line — *what* to do, not *why* it is being done.

Lawyers can perceive reality this way, but they must also envision how a court might interpret the situation in later litigation. Courts depend on evidence. Evidence depends both on the recollections of individuals and, obviously, upon what is written. What is written will be more difficult to refute than what is recollected. The lawyer worries about the reconstruction of a transaction in court — a reconstruction that may happen years after the actual events. If the case is tried before a jury, the jurors not only will know nothing about the specific transaction but, most likely, will have no experience in similar transactions. By the time of trial, parties may have poor recollections and of course will have every incentive to make themselves look good and somebody else look bad. Recollections are likely to be further distorted by recrimination and self-justification.

Both the management's presentation and the board's decision therefore must be imprinted in an institutional memory. Apart from the need for subsequent reconstruction is the value of structured deliberation in the actual decision. The directors are part of a process that must yield an informed decision. The directors must be provided a balanced and comprehensive presentation of the factors relevant to whether a company should be sold. A better-reasoned and more disciplined decision is reached. Form creates substance.

Presentations to the board should be carefully organized and coordinated between management and the outside experts. All relevant material areas of inquiry should be covered in a concise and informative fashion. The advantages *and disadvantages* of a recommended course of action should be explored. The environment must be one of openness and thoroughness, with questions encouraged. Management's and advisers' answers should be thoughtful and candid. The minutes should reflect the nature and extent of the deliberations. This does not mean a verbatim transcript; it does mean a recital of the key issues addressed — the company's forecasts, its financial condition, the benefits and disadvantages of the proposed transaction, and the company's ability to operate as an independent entity. Any written presentation by the investment bankers should be an exhibit to the minutes.

When doing so is feasible, information about the prospective transaction should be furnished to directors in advance of the meeting. If that is not possible, key documents should be carefully reviewed at the meeting and sufficient time provided for such a review. The advice of outside investment bankers, although not required, should be obtained in evaluating an extraordinary transaction. If practicable, the advice should be in a written opinion.

That there is a tight timetable does not excuse uninformed board action. The bidder's time demands are a part of the issues that the board must address. If extension of the meeting over successive days is necessary, the meeting must be extended.

If a bidder proposes to restrict the company's ability to shop for higher bids, or seeks to limit the company's opportunity to obtain a better price, the proposal must be weighed very carefully. These arrangements may be perfectly appropriate, but they require careful financial and legal analysis.

Carrying out a legal responsibility, such as that of a director, entails the risk of legal liability. The law pretends to be uniformly effective in enforcing legal responsibility. In fact, the law is usually enforced only in an episodic and exemplary way. *Smith* v. *Van Gorkom* in an episode of law enforcement. Once in a while, some directors must be taken out and hanged, their bodies left on the gibbet, so that all other directors will remember that they must be good directors. As Samuel Johnson said, "Depend upon it, Sir, when a man knows he is to be hanged in a fortnight, it concentrates his mind wonderfully."

Directors should be given the maximum protection afforded by the law. The company should adopt, or seek shareholder approval of, provisions that limit director liability, as permitted by recent changes to state corporation laws. In addition, directors should be covered by the broadest permissible indemnity agreements or bylaw provisions. The company should have officer and director liability insurance that is kept current. Otherwise directors may not be willing to serve.

o   o   o

The litigation was remanded to the Delaware Chancery Court to determine the amount of damages. Trial was scheduled for October 7, 1985. However, in July 1985, after complicated negotiations initiated by the defendants, Trans Union and the board settled out of court. The directors denied all charges of wrongdoing but agreed to pay $5.5 million in compensation to the shareholders — less than $1.44 per share — and $18 million in attorneys' fees, a total of $23.5 million. Only $10 million was covered by directors' liability insurance, so the nine directors of Trans Union agreed to pay the remaining $13.5 million. According to the *New York Times,* this sum was provided by Pritzker.

What became of Trans Union? Less than a year after the merger, Bruce Chelberg, Trans Union's president and chief operating officer, became senior vice president, international, for IC Industries, Inc. — where Van Gorkom was a director and whose chief executive officer was former Trans Union director William Johnson. A few months later, Jack Kruizenga, once head of Trans Union's tank car division, was recruited to run Pullman Standard Inc., a railcar industry giant that Kruizenga proceeded to overhaul. In September 1982, on the recommendation of Van Gorkom's good friend George Shultz, President Ronald Reagan appointed Van Gorkom under secretary for management of the State Department. The *New York Times* reported that Shultz wanted a "trusted confidant" in this State Department senior management position.

How did the Pritzkers make out with their purchase? Reporting five years after the fact on Pritzker's purchase of Trans Union, the *New York Times* stated, "The deal has put a damper on Marmon's enviable earnings. . . . High interest rates payable on the $550 million that the Pritzkers borrowed to finance the acquisition, and a slump in tank car sales, aggravated problems already being generated at Marmon by the recession."

Did the directors sell Trans Union for less than it was worth? No one knows for certain, any more than anyone can know the true motives of Trans Union's management. But the key to understanding the fate of the nine directors of Trans Union — and the vagaries of corporate law — is that they were "hanged" on the issue of process, not of price. From the perspective of the law of corporate governance, there is no such thing as simply a result. The law's essential concern is process, even where the board's decision may be right on its merits. Process can be reviewed and improved. The decision itself is always a matter of dispute.

The "true" value of Trans Union's shares at the time the deal was struck, for example, can never be determined. Prices for buying and selling cannot be determined by hindsight, any more than there can be betting on races after the running is over. Moreover, as the moment of the decision to sell recedes further into the past, it becomes more difficult to reconstruct the facts at the time. Faltering memory and intervening occurrences blur impressions of the original event.

Courts are deeply mindful that proof of disputed facts is to an important extent conjectural. This is true even when courts firmly recite "the facts," as they did in the Trans Union decision. The dissenting judges, and certainly the directors and their lawyers, thought the facts were quite otherwise — that at the time and under the circumstances, the amount offered for the shares was "fair," or at least within the range of what could be said to be fair. The legal system imposed its decision as to what the facts were and therefore whether the offer was fair, but it could not be sure its conclusion was right. Even in criminal cases — even in criminal cases involving capital offenses — the most the law requires is proof beyond a reasonable doubt. In civil cases, the law will grant or deny judgment on the basis of conclusions resting on nothing more than a preponderance of evidence: the merest tipping of the balance.

The law thus decides finally but without necessarily being right. As former Justice Robert Jackson of the United States Supreme Court once said of courts and judges: "We are not final because we are infallible, but we are infallible only because we are final."

Recognizing that this is all the law can do in the way of fact-finding puts the director's legal responsibilities in a very different light. The "facts," as the courts may eventually find them, are simply a judicial "judgment call." But if this is true, what can directors do to prevent adverse judicial judgment calls about the directors' own judgment calls? The answer turns out to be at the same time simple and complex. Simply put, the director has to consider not only what decisions are made but the process by which they are made. The answer is complex because a director's responsibilities to shareholders are themselves complex — involving the full intricacies of finance, business, management, law, intuition, and power.

PART I

∘ ∘ ∘

THE POWER STRUCTURE, SHARK REPELLENTS, AND THE POISON PILL

CHAPTER 1

o   o   o

"To Direct and Superintend the Affairs of the Corporation"

I T WOULD be nice to say that the modern business corporation, as a tool for the accumulation and exercise of economic power, was invented one fine day in the eighteenth century, just like the steam engine. But the modern business corporation was no more invented in a day than was the steam engine or the electric light. It emerged from earlier forms by stages of development and after adjustments responding to failure. Like the typical successful business, the successful form of business organization — the modern corporation — is the product of creative response to failure.

The modern corporation has deep historical roots. One goes back to the Middle Ages and before, ever since substantial trade in goods has been carried out over a distance. This is the merchant caravan or, at sea, the convoy. In a caravan, merchants gained the strength of numbers and organization against predators such as highwaymen, toll collectors, locally entrenched business competitors, monopolistic suppliers, and tax-hungry politicians. The Silk Route from China to Damascus was traversed by such caravans, and so were the routes to leading market cities in Europe. In Renaissance Europe, the famous East India companies organized by the British, Dutch, and French provided merchant venturers with strength in oceangoing ventures.

Another root of the modern business corporation is foreign

exchange banking. The foreign exchange bankers, such as the Genoese, Florentines, and later the Fuggers of Germany, could provide payment in City I for goods delivered in City II, or credit in City III for manufacturing for a market in City IV. They provided transaction lubricants for the merchant traders — credit, accounting, risk assessment, market information. Credit accommodations became banking arrangements, and moneylenders evolved into bankers. Banks were one of the earliest forms of the modern business corporation, and the early forms of other types of corporate enterprise were among the banks' first customers. Corporate budgeting, allocation of capital, cash flow control, managerial accounting, and "bottom line" responsibility are now taken for granted. These techniques are essentially internal banking transactions.

The special-purpose government agency is a third root of the modern business corporation. Before the nineteenth century, a corporation could be formed only with special royal authorization, for the purpose of accomplishing a government purpose. In English law, from which our American law derives, the corporate charter was granted by "letters patent" — meaning a public, or patent, grant of authority. Usually the grant included a monopoly, such as the right to operate a ferry or to engage in a particular trade. This procedure of granting an exclusive right (i.e., a legal monopoly) is the origin of modern patents for inventions and also for the form of appointments to public office: The standard form of authorization is an "open" letter typically beginning: "All to whom these presents shall come, Greeting."

In the seventeenth century, letters patent in the form of a corporate charter were granted only for special public purposes — to build a road or a canal, to drain marshland, to trade with China and on the way find the Northwest Passage, or to colonize in the Caribbean or North America. The Virginia Company, which founded Jamestown in 1607, was a special-purpose corporation chartered by the crown and financed by private subscription. Pennsylvania originally was organized on the basis of a charter to William Penn, for the benefit of his

Quaker coreligionists; Maryland was similarly organized by Lord Baltimore for his Catholic coreligionists. There were all kinds of similar corporations established in England and later in this country. The Erie Canal was a special-purpose corporation, and so were most of the early American railroads. In concept, each was designed to meet a particular public need — like modern-day Amtrak or NASA.

What is now private corporate enterprise thus originated as public corporate enterprise. In each case, the corporate charter conferred the advantages of formal organization, authority to accumulate capital, and government recognition. The charter usually named the new entity, designated its founding governors or trustees, and specified its powers — essentially the enterprise's constitution. The advantage in the corporate form of organization was that it provided orderly governance for group efforts and facilitated large accumulation of capital because relatively small sums could be raised from a large number of subscribers — thus diversifying investor risk. It also had the advantage of stability over time because a corporation, unlike a personal proprietorship, did not die with its founder.

Another institutional forebear of the modern business corporate form paradoxically is the church corporation, which had its origins in Roman law carried forward through canon law. There were two basic kinds of church corporations, the diocese and the religious order. The diocese was a geographical corporation, centered on a city or town and headed by a bishop. The diocese evolved from the early informal organization of the Christian church and assumed greater formality after Christianity became the state religion of the Roman Empire. The religious order was a residential or associational corporation, generally centered on a monastery or convent and headed by an abbot or similar official. Both kinds of church corporation involved legal concepts that later proved convenient for business corporations.

The basic concept is that the corporation is distinct from and exists beyond the lives of its members. Thus, the bishop may die or be deposed, but the diocese as a corporation lives on. A related concept is that the entity owns property, participates in transactions, and exists for legal and political purposes independent of any of its individual members. There are some wonderful cases in medieval law involving the question of whether and how an abbey can legally exist when the incumbent abbot has died and his successor has not yet been appointed. This kind of legal problem got worked out — the abbey was held to have continuous existence even though the father figure didn't. Such a solution was then used in dealing with situations in which the mayor of a town had died and was still later carried over to the business corporation; for example, it applies when the chairman of the board or CEO is dismissed.

From at least as early as the sixteenth century, corporations typically had a board of directors, or governors or trustees, as they usually were called. The members of the board normally included notables and nobles — people with clout, just like today. The board selected, supervised, and supported, and if necessary replaced, the chief executive officer.

Originally, the board appointed not only the chief executive officer but also the other principal officers: the vice president, treasurer, and secretary. In legal form, appointment of officers is still done this way, so that the first order of business of the board each year is solemnly to reelect the slate. In time, it became established practice for the CEO to nominate all subordinate officers, a nomination that was tantamount to election. The result is that in the modern corporation the CEO effectively hires, and can fire, all the top-level executives, and controls the hiring and firing of management at all levels. This concentration of authority in the hands of the CEO can be explained in terms of reducing the risks of internal conflict and confusion in corporate policy that would result if authority were structured otherwise.

The combination of board and CEO still is the core of the corporate business organization. It is so common that its powerful organizational characteristics may not be apparent. The members of a board are not dependent on the corporation's business for their livelihood, as are members of a family farming operation or a partnership business. The directors, or at least the independent directors, thus do not have everything at stake in the immediate success of the business. Also, a board of directors does not dissolve if one of its members dies or retires, whereas a partnership may have to be reconstituted if that happens. A board does not express the idiosyncratic viewpoint of one individual but can act and "think" only by communications among its members. These organizational characteristics tend to promote stability, objectivity, and rationality. Of course, they can result in "group think," where each person reaches a conclusion because everyone else has.

The board supervises the chief executive officer of the corporation but does not itself act for the corporation. Action by the corporation is taken by the CEO and subordinates reporting to him. If the CEO cannot do the job, he will be replaced. The clear division between general supervisory authority, which is held by the board, and general managerial authority, which is held by the CEO, took a long time to evolve. However, from the sixteenth century onward, the basic structure was revealed in the fact that ultimate authority under the corporate charters rested in the board and not a single individual. Early corporate charters that are still operative speak that way in so many words — "the President and Fellows of Harvard University," for example.

The corporate organization also introduced the beginnings of another feature of the modern business corporation: people who are employees rather than proprietors, but who have high status and are well paid. The CEO of a modern corporation has professional and community standing equal or superior to that of independent businessmen and of professionals such as bankers and lawyers. Yet the CEO is an employee, as are other members of corporate management. Members of corporate management hold their positions on the basis of continuing performance, under authority of the board. They are hired hands. In the modern era we are so accustomed to identifying people's places according to their performance that we forget that the relationship used to be the other way around. Before the capitalist revolution, people were born into their places in society — peasant, artisan, gentleman, lord, or king — and then performed as best they might. Now the corporation makes performance, all the way to top management, the basis of place, rather than place being the basis of performance.

Today, the board members themselves also typically have earned their places by performance. Of course, there still are many who made it to the board by inheritance, either of the position or of the money that makes the position possible. However, most independent directors — directors who are not employees of the company — have established themselves through some other business or professional capacity. A large percentage of independent directors are CEOs or the equivalent in outside businesses or nonprofit organizations. And the "inside directors" — directors who are employees of the company — have to maintain performance as employees as a condition of remaining on the board. This goes double for the CEO, who in modern practice is not only a member of the board but its chairman.

One characteristic of the modern corporation that is now considered essential, which did not exist in the beginning, is the limited liability of shareholders. Everyone today knows that when buying a share of stock, the investor risks what he invests but does not risk more. Specifically, a shareholder does not risk becoming liable for debts of the corporation if it not only loses its assets but, like Penn Central or Johns Manville, piles up huge liabilities as well. An original shareholder's liability is "limited" to the amount of the original subscription price of the corporation's stock. When that amount has been paid, neither the original stockholder nor any purchaser of the stock is liable any further.

Limited liability allows investors in a business enterprise to undertake a bounded risk — their up-front investment. In contrast is the risk assumed by a proprietor of a business or a general partner in a partnership who commits not only an upside investment but also assumes legal responsibility for downside liabilities of the venture that may ensue if it fails. Limited liability through the corporate form of enterprise encourages people to invest in businesses that they may not know much about and whose affairs they cannot closely monitor; this protective incentive facilitates a wider market for corporate securities.

However, limited liability of stockholders was not characteristic of business corporations until the nineteenth and twentieth centuries. Indeed, until legal changes were made following the Great Depression of 1929–37, the shareholders of many corporations were assessable for unpaid corporate liabilities, like members of a club. The assessment rate typically was once or twice the par value of shares, so that a holder of a $100 par value share could be assessed $100 or $200 to meet corporate debts. (That is one reason par value used to mean something.) In today's world, limited liability is a central concept of the corporate form of business and is now imitated in limited partnerships with widely held units. But originally the key feature of the corporation was that it facilitated rationally disciplined management and stability over time. This increased the opportunity to make money. As Samuel Johnson said, in a prospectus for a brewery business: "We are not here to sell a parcel of boilers and vats, but the potentiality of growing rich beyond the dreams of avarice."

There was another basic change in American corporation law occurring in the nineteenth century. Corporations were allowed to be in more than one business and, as a means toward that end, to take over another corporation by merger. Corporate charters in the eighteenth century specifically limited the business or activity in which the corporation could engage. Also it was the rule, originating in English law, that a corporation could not itself own another corporation. Both limitations reflected fear on the part of governments of the time that corporations could get out of hand and become domains unto themselves. Such fears were not unreasonable, given the weak investigatory and control mechanisms available to eighteenth-century governments. For example, the British East India Company got so involved in governing India that in 1784 Parliament had to require that it be taken over by the government. The Bank of the United States, created by authority of Congress in 1791, had its corporate existence terminated in 1836, owing to fear of its power.

The original prohibition of diversification and mergers, however, imposed inflexibility in management and inhibited economies of scale. An illustration is in the development of railroads. Originally, railroad companies both in England and in this country were organized like toll roads — they ran in a direct route from one city to another (thus, the old Boston & Worcester, and the New Haven & Hartford ran directly between those respective pairs of cities). If goods had to be shipped beyond those points on either end, they had to go over to another line with another schedule. It soon became evident that more efficient transportation could result if interconnecting lines were strung together and if intersecting lines could be organized on the principle of hub and spokes. Such an integration of operations often could be achieved only by either merging one railroad corporation into another or creating a new holding company corporation that would control both.

The same principle could apply in integration of manufacturing operations, for example, where a steel company could acquire iron- and coal-mining companies to supply itself with raw materials. The Standard Oil Company, John D. Rockefeller's great corporate combine, involved integration both of transportation (pipelines and tank cars) and manufacturing (production of petroleum products from oil field through refining). Theoretically, such integrations could have been accomplished by transfer of assets from the target corporation to the acquiring corporation. Practically, however, it was often much easier to transfer the corporations themselves. By the end of the nineteenth century, this technique came to be legally permissible in almost all states for almost all types of businesses. (There were, and still are, special restrictions on the corporate structure of banking corporations and other kinds of financial institutions.)

All these historical sources contribute to the modern legal concept of a business corporation. The concept includes the right to form a private government, an important political freedom. It includes the separate legal identity of the entity as distinct from its members; permanent existence; separation of investment from management; and division of authority between board and management. Today it includes limited liability on the part of investors and the right to diversify and merge.

The business corporation melds these ingredients into a complex legal idea. When all is said and done, a corporation *is* simply a legal idea. The nature of the concept is suggested by Justice Joseph Story's famous description in the *Dartmouth College* case, decided by the United States Supreme Court in 1819.

The *Dartmouth College* case involved the question of whether the charter for Dartmouth College, issued in 1769 by King George III, could be changed without the college's consent. The charter originally provided for twelve trustees, who could elect their successors as vacancies occurred. In 1816, over the opposition of the trustees, the New Hampshire legislature adopted a statute enlarging the board to twenty-one, providing a board of overseers with veto power over action by the trustees, and empowering the state's governor and council to elect successor trustees as necessary.

The legal question was whether the state of New Hampshire could thus reconstitute the Dartmouth corporate structure. The Supreme Court held that, since a corporate charter is a contract between the corporation and the state, revising the charter would violate the restriction in the Constitution that no state may pass a law "impairing the obligation of contracts." In reaching this conclusion, the court gave a classic legal definition of a corporation:

A collection of individuals united in one collective body, under a special name, and possessing certain . . . capacities in its collective character which do not belong to the natural persons composing it. Among other things it possesses the capacity of perpetual succession, and of acting by the collective vote or will of its component members. . . . It is, in short, an artificial person, existing in contemplation of law, and endowed with certain powers . . . as distinctly as if it were a real personage.

If there seems something gothic in this — an echo of a vesper in the time of Pope Innocent III — there is reason.

o   o   o

The legal duties of corporate directors as we know them today were established in 1742, in the case of *The Charitable Corporation* v. *Sir Robert Sutton*. The case arose out of classic facts of corporate misgovernance, the total failure of directors' oversight of management. Since then the legal rules have been enormously elaborated into volumes and volumes of court decisions, reams of statutes, government controls, stock exchange regulations, accounting standards, and legal and business treatises. But the legal fundamentals are still much the same. All the quotations from the opinion by the English Court of Chancery could have come, with little change, from a present-day decision by the Delaware Supreme Court.

The lawsuit in *Charitable Corporation* v. *Sutton* was on behalf of the corporation against the directors for "breach of trust, fraud, and mismanagement." As the court observed, the corporation "took its rise from a charter of the crown." According to the charter, the stated purpose of the Charitable Corporation was to "assist poor persons with sums of money by way of loan, to prevent their falling into the hands of pawnbrokers, etc." This was before Adam Smith explained the beneficial effects of business competition in *The Wealth of Nations,* published in 1776. In those days, new enterprises were thought to create economic instability and to jeopardize existing businesses. Some specific public purpose therefore was required in order to obtain a corporate charter.

Today we recognize the public benefits resulting from competition between private businesses and assume that public good will result from new corporate enterprises. However, special authorization — a "certificate of public convenience and necessity," as stated in the *Charitable Corporation* case — is still required to obtain a charter for corporations specially "affected with the public interest," such as banks, public utilities, and insurance companies. The Charitable Corporation was the kind of enterprise that even today would require such special authorization, being essentially a bank "to assist poor persons with sums of money by way of loan." Thus, it was similar to modern-day credit unions, small loan companies (which are supposed to enable small lenders to stay out of the clutches of bankers), farmers' loan banks, and the Small Business Administration. Governments always profess solicitude for small borrowers.

As originally organized, the Charitable Corporation was capitalized at £20,000 — a substantial sum at the time. In 1724, after the corporation had been launched, the capitalization "was enlarged to £100,000, in 1728, to £300,000, and in 1730, £600,000." Said the judge, Lord Chancellor Hardwicke, "I cannot help observing . . . that this deviation from the original fund, was a handle for all the mischiefs which happened afterwards."

The Charitable Corporation's business plan, as we now would call it, was to be a benign pawnbroker. The company would lend money on the basis of articles of property taken as security, issuing the corporation's promissory notes for the amount of the loans. Thus, the borrower would make a pawnshop pledge in return for which the corporation issued its "paper," essentially like modern corporate debentures. Obviously, success in such a venture depended on keeping track of the security received in return for the notes being issued. Every corporate note would put the corporation at greater risk if the pledged property was insecure. As things turned out, the arrangements were insecure.

The company had three officers in charge of the warehouse where the pledged items were stored. "One key of the warehouse was to be in the custody of the *warehousekeeper*, and another in the *cashier's* possession, and a third in the *bookkeeper's*, that each might be a check upon the others. There was another officer, called the *surveyor of the warehouse*, whose business it was to examine all the pledges taken in."

The corresponding responsibilities in a modern corporation would be those of chief executive officer, treasurer, chief of accounting, and auditor. Every corporate enterprise requires operations management, operations control, financial management, and financial control.

As the judge sadly observed, "It has happened that the most important of these rules was broke through. . . . The cashier was ordered to deliver over the key. . . . The surveyor of the warehouse was discharged. . . . The whole power of pledging, etc., developed upon the warehousekeeper and two of his assistants."

Modern accounting records and procedures for verifying inventory protect against these kinds of risk. But these modern procedures became standard only after the famous McKesson & Robbins defalcation in the 1930s. The president of Mc-Kesson & Robbins, like the warehousekeeper of the Charitable Corporation, set up a system whereby he personally controlled a set of purchasing accounts. Through these accounts, McKesson & Robbins for several years paid out large sums for what its records showed was inventory in a warehouse in Montreal. Only later was it discovered that in Montreal there was no inventory but only a clerk, who had been employed by the president. The clerk's job was to submit fictitious invoices to McKesson & Robbins, to record fictitious inventory in the fictitious warehouse, and to remit real cash to the president. The president was much admired for taking only a modest salary while still being able to live rather well.

In *Charitable Corporation* v. *Sutton* the warehouse security system got out of control, but that was not the worst of it. "The most destructive method was advancing money several times upon old pledges, which were not worth more than the first sum lent, or else giving credit upon imaginary pledges."

Much of the money was lent to the warehousekeeper himself, "so that he might be said to be both borrower and lender"; in other words, self-interested dealings with the corporation by the warehouseman—chief executive officer, John Thompson. Also, two of Thompson's assistants "were permitted to act as brokers for the borrowers"; in other words, employees having undisclosed business interests in transactions with the corporation.

In the way of corporate misgovernance, *Charitable Corporation* v. *Sutton* had it all: violation of the regulatory limitations in the corporate charter; self-interested dealing by high-level executives; rip-offs by lower-echelon employees; failure of inventory control; and huge financial commitments unmet and unmanageable. "The loss which ensued from this mismanagement is prodigious, for . . . the money lent was £385,000, whereas the value of the goods pledged was not worth more than £35,000, so that the loss to the corporation is not less than £350,000."

The question then was, as it always is: Who is ultimately responsible for management's incompetence and self-interested dealing? For the failure to control lower employees? For the failure to comply with government regulations on the business? As Lord Hardwicke said in the *Charitable Corporation* case, "The material consideration for me is, from what causes, and from what persons, this loss may be said to arise."

Of course Thompson, the chief executive officer, was responsible. But he had "run away out of the kingdom in order to avoid justice" and possibly had taken the money with him. However, the directors of the Charitable Corporation were still around — the "committee-men," they are called, evidently an executive committee acting on behalf of the investors. They were the defendants, inevitably, and the charges against them have a familiar ring: "The grounds . . . against the committee-men are these: That they have been guilty of manifest breaches of trust, or at least of such supine and gross negligence of their duty, and so often repeated, that it will amount to a breach of trust."

First, the directors failed to comply with stated corporate procedures. "The by-law prescribes, that when notes were to be issued by the cashier, they should be signed by one of the committee-men, and intended as a check upon the warehousekeeper and cashier." In other words, failure to comply with legal requirements in official corporate action. "Several notes have been issued, without observing this rule, which is an express contravention of the by-law."

Second, the directors failed to monitor the corporation's financial procedures. "A new loan is made upon the same pledge. . . . It is not in the nature of the thing possible to suppose that the same person wanting to reborrow could replace the first money lent; and therefore at the outset was plain and obvious fraud."

Third, Thompson was allowed to make loans that benefited himself. A loan to an officer "is such a notorious fraud, or at least gross inattention . . . that, I shall direct those who shall appear to be guilty of it to make good the loss."

The next set of charges concerned "taking off all checks upon Thompson, and making several orders to put it in the power of Thompson . . . to commit those frauds." The law traditionally calls this misfeasance or nonfeasance, as distinct from malfeasance. The Trans Union board was charged with the same kind of inattention, except that the transaction in that case was not fraudulent but said to be underpriced. In the *Charitable Corporation* case there was a similar set of charges, which the judge put under the Latin heading *crassa neglegentia*. *Crassa* means "thick, dense, or solid" and corresponds to the modern legal concept of "gross." The Latin *neglegentia* needs no translation.

The *Charitable Corporation* case laid down principles that generally have held ever since. Lord Hardwicke said: "I take the employment of a director to be of a mixed nature: it partakes of the nature of a public office, as it arises from the charter of the crown. But it cannot be said to be an employment affecting the public government. . . . Therefore committee-men are most properly agents to those who employ them . . . to direct and superintend the affairs of the corporation."

In other words, being a corporate director is an agency responsibility in the nature of a public trust. The concept has since been restated, but in twentieth-century language the concept remains essentially the same. For example, the Comment to §35 of the 1971 edition of the Model Business Corporation Act Annotated, reflecting the opinion of leading corporation lawyers, stated: "The board is commonly charged with the duty and responsibility of managing the business and affairs of the corporation, determining corporate policies, and selecting the officers and agents who carry on the detailed administration of the business."

The law of corporate governance thus has remained substantially the same for more than two hundred years. During that time the key change has been emergence of the large business corporation, since small incorporated businesses still operate much as they did a century ago. In the large modern corporation, the business is run by salaried management under the authority of directors who themselves have at most a small fraction of stock ownership. This was the change clearly noted more than fifty years ago, by Adolph Berle and Gardiner Means in *The Modern Corporation and Private Property*. But the legal rules formally defining the directors' responsibilities have remained essentially unchanged.

Nor has any subsequent legal formulation changed the implications of the rules. One implication of the "agency" concept is that the directors act on behalf of the stockholders and can be called to account for failure to carry out that responsibility. Under principles of agency law, if the directors act in an evidently improper way (or fail to act in a proper way), the stockholders can demand that the directors rectify the situation. In shorthand, this procedure is called the stockholders' demand. If in response the directors do not rectify the situation, the stockholders can bring suit on behalf of the corporation to require that the directors do so. This is the stockholders' derivative suit. In essence, it is a suit by the owners against the custodians. Any shareholder of a modern corporation has authority to bring a so-called derivative lawsuit in the name of the corporation against directors and officers for breaching their duties of loyalty and of reasonable care.

The modern stockholder suit can also be a morality play, whereby the self-styled trusting investor can castigate the directors for their failures and shortcomings. Politically ours is a populist society, many of whose citizens think corporate managers and directors are malefactors of great wealth who lord it over employees, manipulate stocks and bonds, shut plants, pollute the environment, and take big salaries doing it. On the other side, directors and officers bitterly resent being required to justify themselves before possibly mediocre judges and juries at the insistence of a carping lawyer whom they see as a self-serving former ambulance chaser. When corporate directors and officers are presented through the accusations and inquisitions of a derivative suit, they feel like the intellectuals forced into village confessionals during China's Cultural Revolution.

But the modern stockholders' derivative suit has a respectable legal ancestry. If the stockholders of the Charitable Corporation had found out beforehand that Thompson had kept the only key to the warehouse; that he was lending money to himself; and that huge financial liabilities were being incurred — they could have demanded action by the directors. If the directors had taken action, Thompson might not have been able to "run away out of the kingdom." Both the stockholders and the directors would have been better off. On the other hand, if the directors had not responded to the stockholders' demand, the stockholders could have obtained an injunction to impose some "checks upon Thompson." And again both stockholders and directors would have been better off.

But what happens when the water is already over the dam? Where the damage has already been done, ordinarily there is no use looking to the corporate officers and employees to make good the losses. They may have taken off for a distant destination. If they are still in town, they may have no money, in which case their potential financial liability is merely legal theory. If the stockholders cannot get satisfaction from the management for fraud or mismanagement, from whom can they get it?

Inevitably, when the money has gone, the stockholders look to the directors. If the directors have participated in intentional wrongdoing, they are personally liable without much question. Directors who help management or employees in illegal self-interested dealing or reckless dissipation of assets in effect are aiding and abetting embezzlement. A director's personal involvement in wrongdoing to the corporation, if proven by the facts, does not present complicated issues of business ethics or personal morality. It also does not present complicated issues of law. Under the law, that kind of involvement by a director results in liability for damages and may result in criminal liability on the basis of such regulations as the securities laws and the mail fraud law.

But what about situations where the directors have simply been inattentive? That was the accusation in the Trans Union case. No one said that the directors stood to gain themselves or that they helped Van Gorkom in helping himself to an improper benefit. The charge was that the directors did not pay close enough attention to what Van Gorkom was proposing for the corporation. That also was the basic charge against the "committee-men" in *Charitable Corporation* v. *Sutton*. That is, they were charged with *crassa neglegentia* — gross negligence.

As Lord Hardwicke observed, outlining what the evidence might specifically prove:

> In this respect they may be guilty of acts of commission or omission. . . . Where acts are executed within their authority . . . in such cases though attended with bad consequences, it will be difficult to determine that these are breaches of trust. For it is by no means just in a judge, after bad consequences have arisen . . . to say that they foresaw at the time what must necessarily happen.

"Bad consequences" thus were not in themselves a basis for personal liability. Nor are they today. As the American Law

Institute, an organization that clarifies and simplifies the law, has said in its draft of *Principles of Corporate Governance and Structure:* "The critical time for the assessment of the performance of a director or officer is the time of the alleged dereliction. His performance should not be judged in the harsh light of subsequent events."

What about nonattendance to duty? Lord Hardwicke observed: "If some persons are guilty of gross non-attendance, and leave the management entirely to others, they may be guilty by this means of the breaches of trust that are committed by others."

That is still the law, although it necessarily remains uncertain what is meant by "gross non-attendance." However, there are clear cases, such as the conduct of the directors of the Charitable Corporation and those involved in the *Francis* case in New Jersey in 1981.

The *Francis* case involved a family corporation engaged in the insurance brokerage business. The father had built up the corporation, and his sons took it over upon his retirement. After the father's death, the mother became the largest stockholder and continued as a member of the board. The sons began bigger payouts to themselves than the business was earning. To cover, they designated these payouts "loans," which theoretically would be repaid to the corporation. Over the course of four years, while the net income of the business fell from $1.5 million per year to $550,000, the "loans" mounted from $1.8 million to more than $10 million. At that point, the corporation went bankrupt, owing millions to its creditors.

Since the sons by then had virtually no assets, the trustee in bankruptcy sued the mother for allowing the sons to deplete the corporation's assets. Such a suit by a trustee in bankruptcy is essentially similar to a stockholders' derivative suit — the trustee sues as representative of the bankrupt corporation, instead of the stockholders. However, the ultimate beneficiary of such a suit will not be the corporation (which is defunct) nor its stockholders (whose investment has been dissipated) but the corporation's creditors (who have not been paid).

The mother's situation was pitiful. Although a member of the corporation's board, she had no idea what was going on. The board meetings were perfunctory — relating "almost exclusively to the election of officers and adoption of banking resolutions and a retirement plan." There were no outside audits of the corporation's books, and its annual financial statements "were simple documents, consisting of three or four 8½ × 11 inch sheets." Also, after her husband died, she "was old, was grief-stricken over the loss of her husband, sometimes consumed too much alcohol, and was psychologically overborne by her sons."

The court nevertheless held her liable for the losses from the "loans."

> Generally directors are accorded broad immunity . . . [However,] as a general rule, a director should acquire at least a rudimentary understanding of the business of the corporation. . . . Directors are under a continuing obligation to keep informed about the activities of the corporation. . . . The sentinel asleep at his post contributes nothing to the enterprise he is charged to protect.

It was this concept that the Delaware Supreme Court applied against the Trans Union directors, although the directors' failure "to keep informed" in that case was much more debatable.

But exactly what is the duty "to keep informed" that determines whether personal financial liability may be imposed on a director? The intense debate among judges and lawyers over this issue has troubled and baffled corporate officers and directors.

However, it is not a new legal issue. Lord Hardwicke's 1742 opinion in *Charitable Corporation* v. *Sutton,* addressing the very same question, said: "By accepting a trust of this sort, a person is obliged to execute it with fidelity and reasonable diligence." Hardwicke also said that if there was proved "a supine negligence in all of them," then all directors would be liable, as they would be for "not making use of the proper power invested in them by the charter, in order to prevent the ill consequences."

There are several key terms: *trust, fidelity, not making use of the proper power invested in them, reasonable diligence, supine negligence.* These terms, first used 250 years ago and still used today, involve two concepts.

One is the duty of loyalty, signified by the terms *trust* and *fidelity* — the obligation, in whatever a director does, to put the interests of the corporation before personal interest. The duty of loyalty prohibits self-interested dealing with the corporation of the sort Thompson had engaged in. It prohibits taking advantage of business opportunities coming the company's way for personal rather than corporate gain. It prohibits use of insider information for personal profit.

The other concept is the duty of care. But *how* careful? At least in theory, the law distinguishes several levels of carefulness. On a scale of 1 to 6, these levels of care run from strict liability to fraud.

Level of Care	*Legal Standard*
1.	Assure proper result — liability regardless of fault
2.	High degree of care
3.	"Reasonable diligence"
4.	"Supine negligence" (gross negligence)
5.	Recklessness
6.	Fraud

No one has ever questioned that a director is liable for committing fraud against his corporation, so there is no doubt that there is liability at care level 6. Also, no one has ever said that a director should be liable simply because the corporation hasn't succeeded. In *Charitable Corporation* v. *Sutton*, the court ruled out director liability simply on the basis that the corporation suffered loss. As the New Jersey Supreme Court said in the *Francis* case, "Directors . . . are not insurers of corporate activities." Hence, there is no liability at care level 1 and never has been.

Also, since the *Charitable Corporation* case, it has been generally agreed that directors should be liable for "supine negligence" — gross and persistent inattention to responsibilities, care level 4. This necessarily includes recklessness, which is conscious or self-aware indifference to those responsibilities — i.e., care level 5.

Hence, a director is liable for fraud, recklessness, or gross negligence but is not liable simply if bad results occur. This brings us to the middle of the scale. The uncertainties in the law of directors' liability have been, first, whether it should be at care level 3 ("reasonable diligence") or care level 2 (high care), and, second, how the standard applies to a group of part-time overseers.

Lord Hardwicke referred to "reasonable diligence," implying that the standard is care level 3. But he also referred to "trust" and "not making use of the proper power invested in them." In legal terminology, these terms sometimes connote a special degree of care imposed on a trustee. And elsewhere in his opinion Lord Hardwicke said that corporate directors "are within the case of common trustees."

The *Charitable Corporation* decision thus can be read as saying, because it does say, that a director is liable for:

- "supine negligence," which implies that a director is not liable unless his conduct falls below care level 4.
- lack of "reasonable diligence," which implies that a director is not liable unless his conduct falls below care level 3, the same standard of care one must exercise in riding a horse or driving a car.
- the care required of "common trustees," which traditionally means care level 2.

All in all, the opinion is ambiguous on the critical legal issue as to directors' personal financial liability. Yet the under-

lying general concepts are fairly clear. A director exercises a
fiduciary responsibility (this is the duty of loyalty), which must
be exercised with reasonable attention (this is the duty of care).
And the board's job is not to manage the corporation but to
see that it is properly managed.

o   o   o

The principles of director responsibility laid down more than
two hundred years ago in the *Charitable Corporation* case are
still recognized, with some refinements.

The duty of loyalty requires that a director commit himself
to the interests of the company and to its stockholders as
owners of the company, and not to his own interests. In other
words, the duty of loyalty prescribes the proper *direction* in
which the director's efforts and concerns are supposed to move.
The duty of care prescribes the *quality* of that effort. The same
principles apply to corporate management.

As for the duty of loyalty, it may seem ironic that modern
capitalist enterprise is based on a rule of self-denial. Directors
and officers of a capitalist enterprise have positions that give
them status, access to information, inclusion in the power
network, recognition by peers — all those good things. Yet they
must conduct themselves with primary regard to the interests
of others. First of all are the stockholders, who get profits,
which are supposed to result from corporate performance. The
relevant others also include the creditors, whose claims have
to be serviced and paid, and the employees, whose effort and
loyalty have constantly to be guided and nurtured. Capitalist
enterprise fundamentally is based on peaceful cooperation, not
compulsion — a proposition that Adam Smith demonstrated
but Karl Marx sought to destroy. Peaceful cooperation requires self-control and self-denial, and directors must exercise
both.

The basic principle of loyalty is not complicated. Stealing
from the company is disloyalty in its extreme form. Yet even
mild forms of disloyalty can have very destructive effects, because disloyalty necessarily diminishes profits to shareholders
and almost inevitably demoralizes the organization. This hap-

pened at Chrysler in the 1950s, when top management stole from the company by setting up sweetheart contracts with supplier companies that they controlled. Receiving unjustified compensation is stealing from the company. But what level of compensation is unjustified?

Consider the "golden parachute," a compensation arrangement tied to a change in control of the corporation. A golden parachute often calls for an officer to keep his job following a change in control and provides for generous severance terms if he does not. Is such an agreement a proper effort to keep a valuable employee or to secure a key recruit? A legitimate recognition of the need for stability and loyalty in the management group? Or are golden parachute payments a waste of corporate assets? Are some executives so much better than their competition that they deserve more? After all, how much has Joe Montana been worth to the San Francisco 49ers? Who is to judge what a proper payment is?

Congress evidently thinks it can judge. It has passed tax legislation that penalizes both the company and the executive for payments more than three times the executive's average compensation.

There is no standard compensation schedule for business executives like that in the civil service or in collective bargaining agreements. No two executive positions are exactly alike, and no two corporations are exactly alike. At the extreme, matters of executive and director compensation involve the duty of loyalty to the stockholders' interests, because directors are setting their own compensation and at some extreme, executive and director compensation can be a rip-off. But short of the extreme — and the law allows the board of directors very wide latitude concerning matters of executive compensation — the fairness of a salary or director's fee is a question of judgment. Typically the group authorizing golden parachutes consists of the independent directors, who meet with outside consultants. Again process is the key.

The duty of loyalty also bars a director from using confidential information received in the course of serving on the board.

The same principle applies to corporate management and other employees. "Insider trading" is an example. An insider's use of confidential corporate information to trade in the company's stock violates not only the federal securities acts but also the director's common-law duty of loyalty to the corporation.

The landmark insider case involved Texas Gulf Sulphur. Texas Gulf Sulphur had been exploring for minerals in the backwoods of Ontario. After many unsuccessful efforts that yielded only blank drilling cores — they were looking for ore, not oil — the company's field crew found a pattern in the borings that indicated a big field. If leases were quickly and discreetly obtained, the discovery could be a bonanza.

Word of the find went immediately to top management. The company put out a guarded and ambiguous public statement about the prospects for the drilling. Simultaneously, members of top management bought shares of the company's stock and call options (rights to buy stock in the future) at the still-undisturbed market price. A few days later, as rumors of the ore strike began drifting out of the North Woods, the company put out a statement more fully outlining the scope of the find. The price of the company's stock shot up. The executives stood to realize tidy sums.

But only temporarily. The scenario aroused the suspicions of the Securities and Exchange Commission. In a subsequent suit brought by the SEC, the court applied the rule of the federal securities laws that a director or officer may not use confidential company information for his own benefit. In effect, the executives stole from other shareholders the difference between the stock price before and the stock price after the news of the ore strike. They also stole from the company public confidence in the integrity of the market in its stock. As Lord Hardwicke had said of the chicanery in *Charitable Corporation* v. *Sutton,* "It is such a notorious fraud." The Texas Gulf Sulphur executives had to give back their gains.

The federal securities laws focus on disclosure, which is

intended to be both informative and restraining. Requiring disclosure of the details of management transactions tends to prevent excesses. For example, information filings with the Securities and Exchange Commission are required whenever there is a change in a director's stock ownership. In the annual proxy statement there must be disclosure of director and officer stock holdings in the company and their compensation. In addition, federal law imposes certain substantive restraints, such as requiring the corporate executive to disgorge any profits from buying and selling his own company stock within a six-month period.

The director's other basic duty is to use "reasonable care." Business involves a constant stream of events, any one of which could go wrong. Independent directors by definition are part-time trustees; like members of a school board or town council, they can't be attentive to all or even most of the transactions coursing through the company every day. The modern large corporation is dispersed horizontally all over the world; it is dispersed vertically through layers of divisions and departments; it is dispersed technically into highly specialized departments. Yet the directors are responsible for using reasonable care in supervising the management of these complex operations.

○ ○ ○

The decisions in *Charitable Corporation* v. *Sutton* and the Trans Union case are the bridges over which the law proceeds from one era to the next. Another key bridge in the law of directors' responsibilities was the decision in *Briggs* v. *Spaulding,* decided by the United States Supreme Court in 1891. In that case, involving claims against directors for losses suffered in the management of a bank, the Supreme Court directly relied on the principles stated in *Charitable Corporation* v. *Sutton. Briggs* v. *Spaulding* in turn is a precedent that could still be cited today, nearly another century later. Principles stated 250 years ago thus are brought forward into modern legal vocabulary.

The bank involved in *Briggs* v. *Spaulding* was a proper bank, a bank with a portico, an apparently prosperous bank, of which solid, leading citizens of Buffalo were proud to be directors.

The directors had felt comfortable in leaving the management to the president, meeting but once a year, signing the annual report, approving payment of the dividends. "Mr. Spaulding [one of the directors] . . . testified that he never received any notice to attend directors' meetings; that he had no actual knowledge of the by-laws . . . that he supposed the bank was in a prosperous condition down to the day of its failure."

On October 3, 1881, the president took a one-year leave of absence. In due course, the circumstances offered a possible explanation for his departure:

> The evidence leaves it beyond question that the bank was insolvent on the third of October, 1881, its capital and surplus wholly exhausted, and losses incurred of thousands of dollars beyond that amount . . . the books and papers of the bank were kept in such condition that even the cashier swore he did not suspect anything wrong in the management until April 10, 1882.

Legally, the failure to use reasonable care is "negligence." It resembles the idea of negligence in physical activity — operating a train, driving a car, running a machine — and conveys the picture of preventing somebody from falling asleep at the wheel. Is a director like the driver of a vehicle in that he is negligent if he doesn't have his hand on the wheel? This is where the analogy to negligence in driving an automobile breaks down.

A director, particularly an independent director, who is not a company officer or employee, is not supposed to have his hands on the wheel. That is management's job. The directors are supposed to be overseers of the people who have their hands on the wheel, and they cannot do that if they hold the wheel themselves. It is not that directors are incapable of being managers, for many directors are themselves chief executives of other corporations and are very capable managers. The point is that, if directors *are* management, then in effect there is no one to oversee management.

This distinction between management and directorship is fundamental in corporate governance. Yet the distinction and its implications are difficult to keep clearly in view. Some business executives regard directors as mere decorations — as parsley. On the other hand, actively interested directors can be too actively interested and can become meddlers. Apparently, that is why Chairman Roger Smith of General Motors and Ross Perot disagreed over whether Perot should continue as a member of the GM board.

Academics and professionals such as doctors, lawyers, journalists, and engineers, as well as blue-collar workers on an assembly line, do their work directly and personally. A professional may have assistants, but they are essentially extensions of the professional himself or herself. "Oversight" for a professional means direct continuous monitoring of an assistant whose work is considered the professional's own. Indeed, ethical principles in medicine and law make the doctor and lawyer personally responsible for things done by their assistants.

The concept of oversight by a board of directors is very different. A board of directors functions part-time. This is true even of a board of directors constituted of corporate employees, for employee-directors — inside directors — spend most of their time doing their individual jobs and ordinarily convene as a board only at monthly or less frequent intervals. Independent, or outside, directors by definition perform their responsibilities as such only on an intermittent schedule. By the same token, the people being supervised by a board of directors are themselves independent professionals. Top officers of a corporation are expected to function autonomously, to exercise judgment on their own initiative, and to proceed without immediate supervision.

The directors of a corporation, in exercising reasonable care, therefore are supposed to know generally what is going on but are not supposed to be directly involved in getting it done. To some unavoidable extent, this puts the directors between a rock and a hard place. On one hand, they want to minimize the risk of "surprises" — such as the bad loans in the *Charitable Corporation* and *Briggs* cases or the situation faced by Trans Union's directors, who had not been given the full picture in the company's most critical corporate decision. On the other hand, the directors cannot take over the business, transforming themselves into government by committee and transforming the management into staff assistants. The directors have to be in on major strategic decisions by the corporation, but at a watchful distance in everything else.

The board is something like the captain of an ocean liner who walks around watching and taking salutes to show he is on the job. When the captain is doing his job the best way possible, everyone else is at work and the captain appears to be doing nothing. But is he really keeping an eye on things or is he simply taking salutes?

That is the question a director has to be prepared to answer in court. Since directors' responsibilities involve supervising the use of other people's money, they may have to defend that supervision in court. That defense requires new and compelling arguments if a corporate raider has come knocking at their door.

CHAPTER 2

o   o   o

Shark Repellents, Poison Pills, and Other Corporate Pharmacy

FACED WITH A POTENTIAL TAKEOVER, a board of directors in "superintend[ing] the affairs of the corporation" may take measures to preserve it as an independent public company. Household International, an $8.3 billion diversified holding company, was vulnerable. Corporate raiders were knocking, and one of them was already in the door. He was a Household director, John A. Moran.

Money talks. Since raiders now can finance billion-dollar transactions, no corporation is safe. A raider's all-cash deal can be financed by junk bonds backed up by a target's cash flow and asset base. The enormous expansion in the size of the junk bond market in the 1980s, the availability of credit for acquisitions, and leveraged buyout pools holding more than $15 billion have changed the structure of corporate America. The value of mergers and acquisitions reached a historic high of $82.6 billion in 1982, and new records were set every year thereafter: $122.2 billion in 1984, $179.6 billion in 1985, and $190 billion in 1986. The number of takeovers valued at $1 billion or more quintupled between 1983 and 1986. All told, seventy-five of the one hundred largest mergers in U.S. history occurred since 1981.

Companies have had to focus on ways to defend themselves against unsolicited bids, and defensive planning has become as critical as financial planning and budgeting. Preparation must begin before an actual bid because the key is to deter the raider from acting. Once a takeover is started, the target company has about a one-in-five chance of remaining independent.

A company becomes a takeover target for reasons ranging from strong products to weak management. Sometimes the raider seeks to enter a new line of business. Sometimes a takeover aims to replace ineffective management, with the raider calculating that more money can be made with the same assets but different management. Taking a company apart or putting it together with some other business may result in greater profitability. For example, UAL, Inc., later named Allegis, had a strategy of becoming a "total transportation company" — airlines, hotels, car rentals, all under one roof. Management thought the combination would produce profitable synergy; critics thought it produced confusion. Differences in opinion of this kind translate into different appraisals of the value of a company's stock. And different appraisals of the value of a company's stock can translate into a potential takeover.

"Shark repellents" — measures to ward off potential raiders — are a key part of strategy to preserve a company's independence. The most celebrated shark repellent is the "poison pill." Chicago-based Household International obtained the original prescription.

As early as February 1984, Household International's chairman and CEO, Donald C. Clark, became increasingly concerned about the company's vulnerability as a takeover target. A thirty-year Household veteran, Clark was born and raised in Brooklyn, graduated from Clarkson College of Technology in upstate New York, and had served in the U.S. Army during the Korean War. Toward the end of his two-year military commitment, he answered a blind ad that led into Household International's accelerated training program for college graduates. He worked his way up through Household's financial department, first as assistant treasurer, later becoming treasurer. In the evenings he earned his M.B.A. at Northwestern

University. In 1977, he was named president; in 1982, CEO; and in January 1984, he also became chairman of the board. Clark owned approximately 40,000 shares directly and in employee trust programs, with options to acquire approximately another 100,000 shares — an interest with a total market value of something in excess of $4 million.

Household International's subsidiaries included Household Finance Corporation (HFC), which made loans to blue-collar borrowers and supplied leasing and financing services to commercial customers; National Car Rental; TG&Y, a chain of general merchandise stores in twenty-six states offering "discounts every day"; and Vons Supermarkets in Southern California and Nevada, featuring "low prices you can believe in." Also among Household's holdings was Wallace-Murray Corporation, manufacturer of plumbing equipment and engine parts.

Clark, sensing that "everyone around was doing things," commissioned a "raid preparedness" study by Goldman, Sachs, long-standing investment bankers for Household International; a barometer of the takeover climate; and an extensive list of takeover defenses recently put into play by other companies.

In the 1983 and 1984 proxy seasons, companies that were takeover targets had been mounting ever-greater efforts to obtain shareholder approval of defensive charter amendments, a trend that was to accelerate in the years following. Common among these defensive measures were staggered-term board provisions and fair-price provisions.

A staggered board is one in which only one third of the directors are elected each year; this makes changing a board of directors more difficult. A raider who acquires a majority of the company's stock cannot vote in a majority of the board without two elections of directors. Since a raider cannot be sure of changing management for at least that period, even though he has what otherwise would be controlling ownership, the incumbent board's negotiating position is strengthened.

Fair-price provisions come in various forms. Their aim is to prevent the raider from buying 51 percent of the shares at a good price to get control and then squeezing the remaining shareholders into selling at not so good a price. A fair-price provision typically requires that a shareholder who owns more than 10 percent of the company's stock must, before effecting any transaction with the company (such as a merger), obtain the approval of 80 percent of the shareholders or meet certain fair-price criteria. The fair-price criteria require that shareholders relegated to the back end of a two-step transaction — the second stage following the merger — receive the same price as paid on the front end. Thus minority shareholders are protected in the event that a bidder establishes a significant position in the target and subsequently seeks to acquire the remaining stock.

Clark's understanding of a fair-price amendment was "a charter amendment which would require someone who wanted to take control of Household International to pay all shareholders the same price or the highest price that was paid in a first-step if he goes forward and does a second-step merger."

At one time, a takeover usually involved a single offer to all shareholders. The offerer set the price high enough to induce a majority to sell and then had to pay all other shareholders the same amount. Raiders came to realize they could buy control more cheaply. They would offer one price for the first 51 percent of shareholders who sold but a lower price to those who held out. This is a two-tier offer. A two-tier offer is front end–loaded in that the premium offered in the first phase is greater than the price offered in the second phase involving a merger, when the minority is invited to sell out. It pressures each stockholder to be an early seller. The second step, or back end, in a two-tier offer is called the squeeze-out transaction.

Because they were designed to ward off the "shark" — the corporate raider — these structural defenses came to be known as shark repellents. Shark repellents do not prevent takeovers, but they make it more difficult to carry out stock accumulation programs and partial tender offers. However, the board of the target has powers that can relieve this difficulty. Hence, shark repellents give the board of the target negotiating leverage in dealing with a raider.

Staggered-board and fair-price provisions generally receive stockholder approval. Between December 1982 and June 1984, almost three hundred companies had proposed staggered-board or fair-price charter amendments, more than 94 percent of them receiving approval. Today, most Fortune 500 companies have both a staggered board and fair-price provisions.

The staggered-board, fair-price, and other protective provisions usually require amendment of the corporation's charter, and that in turn requires a shareholders' vote. While the board of directors has the general authority to make decisions for the corporation *and* its shareholders, certain decisions are regarded as so fundamental that the shareholders must vote on them. These include a merger of the company into another corporation and amendment of the corporate charter. One of the great debates in contemporary corporate law is whether other strategically important decisions by the directors should have to be approved by shareholders. The poison pill has been a prime subject of the debate.

In the spring of 1984 Household International had no structural defenses. To evaluate whether its shareholders would approve a fair-price amendment, Household hired Georgeson & Company, a leading proxy solicitation and takeover consultant. After analyzing Household's shareholder profile, Georgeson concluded that, since a large percentage of Household's shareholders were institutional investors, the amendment would barely pass. Georgeson studies showed that many institutional shareholders oppose these provisions as a matter of policy. John Wilcox, Georgeson's managing director, told Clark that getting a favorable vote would require personal visits to institutional holders to convince them of management's integrity. But Clark had only two weeks. As he later observed, "I frankly did not believe we had enough time to do that."

As Wilcox later explained in testimony, as late as the 1970s a typical corporation's shares were held mostly by individuals listed on the company's books and who could be contacted directly. This type of shareholder usually went along with management. But individual shareholders now tended to have their shares in custody of brokers, so that ownership appeared in the corporation's books only in "street names," i.e., the names of the brokers or other custodians. The real job of a proxy solicitor in the 1970s was "to go out and beat the bushes and get the vote." Now, Wilcox commented, "the real meat of our job . . . is to get votes from . . . the street name holders . . . shares held in broker and bank names."

For Wilcox, there had been a shift of ownership "out of the hands of individuals into larger institutional investors, including insurance companies, professional money managers, pension funds. . . . Now most companies have a majority of their shares held by professional investors." According to Wilcox: "Most of these large institutional investors have as their objective short-term gain, and they feel that any provision that may impede a tender offer or a takeover of the company in which they have invested may have a negative impact on their ability to get a short-term increase in their investment. For a number of years the easiest way to make money on Wall Street has been when the stock price of the company that you have invested in increases because of a takeover. It used to be that conservative money managers did not invest in speculative situations. Now, however, takeovers have become relatively respectable, and even very conservatively run investors look at the speculative element as a good possibility for gains."

This accorded with Clark's evaluation. "Institutional holders," said Clark, were very averse "to anything standing in the way of an offering because they thought they had a right to receive offers. But the premium was the beginning and end of the analysis as far as they're concerned."

Moreover, it was strategically risky for Household to go to its shareholders with a fair-price provision. According to Clark, that would be telling the street, "If you guys want to make a move on Household, do it because they're admitting to the world they're vulnerable."

Indeed, Household was being eyed by John Moran, one of its own independent directors. Moran was president of Dyson-Kissner-Moran Corporation (DKM), an investment firm specializing in buyouts and one of Household's largest single shareholders. He had joined the Household board in 1981 as a sequel to Household's acquisition of Wallace-Murray Corp., which Moran had controlled. "As a result of the exchange of shares, they turned out to own about six percent of Household," said Clark, and "we thought, not for that reason alone, but that coupled with the fact that they were sophisticated business people, they would make good board representatives. We started out having two on the board, though we had said only one, but Charlie Dyson was . . . reaching age 72 [mandatory retirement] and as a courtesy we allowed him to come on the board. . . . John was sort of Charlie's choice for the long term." Household's acquisition activity had thus increased its own exposure to an acquisition.

As a director of Household, Moran continually complained that Household shareholders were not getting nearly enough value. In 1984, Household earned a record $234 million, or $4.18 per share, on $8.3 billion in sales. The HFC division was doing well, but operations in car rentals, merchandising, and manufacturing had dragged down earnings. Based on financial studies conducted by DKM, Moran had concluded that Household's stock was significantly underpriced in relation to the company's breakup value. He acquired an additional 400,000 to 500,000 shares of Household on the open market and attempted to interest Clark in a leveraged buyout with management participation. Money would be borrowed on the basis of Household assets, the loan proceeds would be used to buy out existing shareholders, the loan would be paid off by divestiture of some of the divisions, and management would participate in the deal.

The deal would have made Clark very wealthy, yet Clark declined the offer. "Our integrity is so high that we couldn't finance the deal because the price I would consider to be fair [to the stockholders] would not be financeable in the marketplace." According to Clark, Moran had said the company was worth $52 per share while its stock was selling in the mid-$20s and had told him: "Don, we can make a successful bid at $35. We will pre-sell HFC for $2 billion and the rest of the company belongs to us free of charge. It could be handled quickly and quietly. . . . We will make $415 million." Clark informed some members of Household's executive committee about Moran's plan, although Moran had asked him not to do so.

In April and May, trading in Household's stock rose from below 100,000 shares a day to as high as 400,000 or 500,000. Unable to identify the purchaser, Clark was "concerned as to whether or not someone was out there accumulating in the first step of an attempt to take Household International over." Clark again conferred with Goldman, Sachs.

Once companies get into play, a study by Goldman, Sachs showed, few remain independent. For example, during the period January 1976 to October 1983, target companies remained independent only 17 percent of the times. In 43 percent of the cases, the target was acquired by a company other than the initial bidder at a higher price than the initial tender price, as the result of defensive tactics. When asked at trial, "Did Goldman, Sachs comfort you?" Clark replied: "No, not at all. They confirmed what we believed was the situation, that Household . . . was an undervalued situation."

A raider has an unlimited time in which to prepare. When he moves, the target's board has only twenty days to evaluate the offer, develop a defensive strategy, and implement its response. This is the minimum time that a tender offer must be held open, under rules prescribed by the SEC. The clock starts when the offer is published in a newspaper with a national circulation or is mailed to the target's shareholders. Twenty business days translates into one calendar month to top the price set by the bidder or to take defensive action.

Clark indicated he would rather see the company liquidated than "have it go at a bargain price and let someone else break it up." However, Goldman, Sachs advised that liquidation would require time and room to maneuver. It was suggested that Clark consider a poison pill instead. Clark appointed a committee of top officers to consult Martin Lipton in legal matters and Goldman, Sachs in the financial aspects of a strategy to be presented at the Household board meeting scheduled for August 14, 1984. Two weeks before that meeting, Clark, in New York for a Warner Lambert board of directors' meeting, met with Lipton to discuss a share purchase rights plan, commonly referred to as the poison pill.

Poison pills give shareholders the right to buy shares at a special price, or to receive some other benefit, when a hostile bidder tries to take over the company. Unless these shareholder rights are redeemed by the directors and thereby neutralized, they make a takeover prohibitively expensive or "poisonous" for the would-be raider. The directors will redeem the rights only when they consider that the right price is being offered for the shares. The power to neutralize special rights gives the directors a bargaining weapon on behalf of the stockholders.

However, a board of directors may fear that a poison pill sometimes will depress the price of the company's shares. Hence there is risk in adopting such a plan. To put a board of directors in a proper frame of mind, one Wall Street adviser would begin his presentation of a pill with the story of two men who are walking in the woods and who suddenly see a big grizzly bear coming at them. One of them takes off his knapsack, takes out his running shoes, unlaces his hiking boots, and starts putting on his running shoes. The other says, "Dummy, you can't outrun that bear." The first replies, "I don't have to outrun the bear, I only have to outrun you."

One form of poison pill is the warrant dividend plan. This is a dividend to stockholders consisting of a warrant to buy one additional share of common stock or common stock equivalent (such as a participating preferred — which participates in earnings and dividends like common) for each share already held. As issued, the warrants are not represented by certificates and trade automatically with the common stock. They are exercisable when a potential raider acquires a specified percentage of the common stock or starts a tender or exchange offer. In the jargon of takeovers, this event "activates the pill." The price of exercising the warrant is fixed substantially above the stock's current market price on the basis of the estimated long-term value of the stock. Exercise prices range from 100 percent to 500 percent of the then-current market price of the common stock.

The "poison" in the pill operates as follows: A "flip-over" provision entitles the holder to receive common stock worth twice the warrant's exercise price. For example, where the exercise price is $100, the warrant holder is entitled to $200 worth of the acquirer's stock for $100. The resulting cost to an acquirer can be substantial — typically very poisonous. Subsequently, an additional "flip-in" was developed. This gives all shareholders except the raider a right to buy stock from the target at half price if the raider acquires, say, 25 percent of the target's voting shares. A triggering of the flip-in creates enormous dilution to the raider.

Provisions in the warrants authorize the issuer's board to redeem the special rights by buying them back at a nominal cost, ranging from one cent to one dollar per warrant. Redemption may be effected within a fixed number of days — usually ten — after an outsider acquires a specified percentage of the company's stock. This is less time than a bidder normally will need to obtain control of the target's board.

This power to terminate the rights gives the board a strong negotiating device in a takeover situation and was perhaps the most important feature of the plan presented by Lipton to Clark: The plan gave the board total flexibility to redeem the rights; it had a "string on the rights." However, once the redemption period passed, the Household-type pill became non-redeemable. Subsequent pills would, in some cases, permit the board to redeem the rights if the company were to merge with a party other than the raider.

The poison pill is controversial precisely because it affects the nature of the company's shares and yet can be implemented without shareholder approval, whereas stockholder approval generally is required of major changes in corporate financial structure.

A summary of the plan was sent in advance of the August 14 board meeting to all Household's directors, along with articles on takeovers, such as *Fortune*'s " 'Oops! My Company Is on the Block,' " and an invitation to all directors to attend an informal dinner the evening before. On Monday, August 13, Clark held a brief preview with Chicago-area directors. The next day the entire board met. Aside from John Moran, the outside directors included Raymond C. Tower, president and chief operating officer of FMC Corporation, a chemicals, machinery, and equipment manufacturer; Miller Upton, formerly president of Beloit College; Arthur E. Rasmussen, Household's retired chairman and CEO; and John C. Whitehead, then senior partner, Goldman, Sachs. Upton, Rasmussen, and Whitehead knew about Moran's buyout proposal from its inception.

Gordon McMahon and Peter Fahey, both partners of Goldman, Sachs, and Martin Lipton were present at the meeting. Fahey made the primary presentation, discussing the company's performance, shareholder base, book value, and attractiveness at various prices. He also surveyed possible acquirers. Lipton warned that Household's "future and all its constituencies could be decided in less than 30 days." He noted that AVCO, another financial services company, was then the subject of a takeover attempt by Leucadia.

Clark added that executives at Household had received calls from Leucadia, "shopping" pieces of AVCO even before it had taken the company over. Leucadia also had asked John Moran if he were interested in joining the Leucadia group. The matter was discussed with Clark, who asked Moran what he thought. Moran gave no clear response, which led Clark to recall that "John had an inclination to get involved in hostile takeovers."

Lipton explained that a potential acquirer probably would probe the target's receptivity to an acquisition. He suggested that the board should respond "as a collegial body" since individual directors could give off signals that the board as a whole "might not intend."

The defense strategy was fourfold: a declaration by the board that it was in the best long-run interest of the corporation to remain independent; adoption of limitations on special shareholder meetings (at which control issues might be raised); amendment of the company's employee benefit plans (ESOPs) to permit the employee beneficiaries, rather than the trustee of the plan to tender stock held in the ESOP if there was a takeover; and the preferred share purchase rights plan, the poison pill. The first three proposals were blessed by all the directors, including Moran. The rights plan was a different matter.

The forty-eight-page plan had a complexity designed to create uncertainties for a potential acquirer. The summary given to Household's board stated:

> The plan creates rather complicated situations that may be difficult for a potential raider to evaluate. In so doing it may deter a takeover. If the plan did not deter a takeover, the plan would virtually assure that any takeover attempt would be for cash and for all the shares of [Household's] stock. To avoid the dilution to the raider's common stock created by a substantial amount of rights being outstanding following a tender offer, a raider would condition its offer on a very large percentage, 80% to 90%, of the rights being tendered.

Under the plan, each Household shareholder would receive one ten-year right for each common share outstanding. The rights, prior to a triggering event, would be nonexercisable and could not be transferred apart from the company's common stock and would have no voting privileges.

Either of two triggering events would activate the rights. First, if a tender offer for 30 percent of Household's shares was commenced or 20 percent of the shares was acquired, the rights would be issued and would be immediately exercisable to purchase ⅟₁₀₀ share of new preferred stock for $100. The rights could be redeemed by the board for 50 cents per right until the purchase of 20 percent of Household's shares; thereafter the rights could no longer be redeemed by the board. Thus, the rights would not interfere with a negotiated merger or a white knight transaction even after a hostile tender offer had been commenced, except after a 20 percent acquisition.

Second, if a right had not been exercised for the preferred stock and a merger or consolidation thereafter occurred, each right could be exercised to purchase $200 of the common stock of the postmerger corporation for $100. The dilution of the acquirer's capital resulting from this "flip-over" would be, in Lipton's words, "immediate and devastating." It was this flip-over feature that earned the label of poison pill.

The minutes of the Household board meeting record a "pointed exchange" between Lipton and Moran. Moran believed that the plan would entrench management while denying shareholders the opportunity to sell their shares at a premium in a tender offer. Lipton argued that two-tier offers served only the short-range interests of certain speculation-minded shareholders. Since the rights plan would encourage a raider to negotiate with the board, the board could thus protect the interests of "all constituencies of the corporate family." With Clark strongly endorsing the plan, the vote was 14 in favor and 2 against. Moran's vote was negative, as expected.

Less expected was the negative vote of John Whitehead, then co-chairman of Goldman, Sachs, whose representatives presented the plan. However, Whitehead had not previously discussed the plan with his firm. He was concerned not with the concept as such, but its novelty. As he later testified, he believed Household should not be a "guinea pig."

o   o   o

Six days later, on August 20, Moran and DKM filed suit in the Delaware Chancery Court to void the rights plan. They claimed it would preclude any tender offer that did not have prior board approval and thus "take away from the stockholders and vest solely in the board the stockholders' fundamental right to receive and consider proposals for control of the corporation." The SEC and the Investment Company Institute, representing the investment company industry, filed friend-of-the-court briefs supporting Moran, the SEC contending that Household's poison pill would "virtually eliminate hostile tender offers." The United Food and Commercial Workers International Union, representing various employee groups, backed Household International. All corporate financial and legal specialists and many major U.S. corporations were interested observers.

Testifying for Moran were Richard C. Abbott, former head of mergers and acquisitions at Morgan Stanley, and Alan Greenberg, CEO of Bear Stearns. Both said a hostile offer would never be made in the face of the rights plan. Arbitrageurs in particular trade on the basis of their estimates of the likelihood that a deal will be completed rather than upon the market value of the stock. If a tender has to be for 90 to 95 percent of the stock in the first step, arbitrageurs would estimate that the offer will fail and would not take the risk in buying. That would weaken demand for the stock and depress its price.

Moran also had testimony of academic experts. Michael C. Jensen, a University of Chicago free-market economist, testified that the rights plan diminished share value in two respects: first, in loss of the premiums paid in takeover tenders; and second, by weakening pressure on management to be efficient in managing corporate resources.

Jensen concluded that the market price of a target company gained an average of 30 percent in the thirty days surrounding a tender offer. Even in two-tier offers, the "blended premium" — i.e., the premium on a weighted average of the prices in both phases — generally reflected a significant increase over the pre-bid market price. Jensen agreed that small shareholders might be harmed by hostile two-tier tender offers but concluded that overall such offers were beneficial.

Household argued that the rights plan was a reasonable protection of the corporation and its shareholders. A chief witness for Household was Raymond Tower, president of FMC Corporation and an outside Household director not named as a defendant in the case. Tower had direct experience in two-tier tender offers, both as an offerer and as a member of a target board. As a director of Marathon Oil Company during its 1981 battle against Mobil, he testified that the rights plan was preferable to the frenzied last-minute devices resorted to by Marathon; Marathon had to choose between staking its independence on including an antitrust case against Mobil and finally acquisition by a white knight. The rights plan gave the board flexibility "to deal at arm's length with a potential acquiror without resorting to self-destructive devices."

Jay Higgins, head of mergers and acquisitions at Salomon Brothers, and Raymond Troubh, a former partner in Lazard Frères and a director involved in takeover struggles at Warner Communications and Pabst Brewery, also testified in support of the plan. John Whitehead, although he had voted against the plan, testified that he agreed with its substance, even though he objected to its novelty and complexity.

Household also presented evidence of the careful deliberations leading to the plan's adoption. Mitchell P. Kartalia, an outside director and chairman and CEO of Square D Company, testified that the board's review was the most extensive discussion of a single topic in his twelve years on the board. All directors were fully aware that the plan would strongly discourage a hostile two-tier offer. The legal advice from Wachtell, Lipton and from Richards, Layton and Finger, a Delaware firm, was recited.

Following a nine-day trial, the trial court ruled for Household. Moran announced he would appeal.

At a meeting of Household's board held on February 15, the directors, with Moran dissenting, voted not to nominate Moran for reelection as a director at the next annual meeting in May. Moran offered two resolutions: to nominate himself for reelection, and to provide the shareholders an opportunity to express their views regarding redemption of the poison pill. Both failed for lack of a second. Five days later, Moran made a

demand on Household for a list of shareholders "to permit
Moran and DKM to communicate with other stockholders on
matters relating to their interests." Household complied with
Moran's demand. "Thereafter," said Clark, "he did absolutely
nothing."

                               o   o   o

Nine months later, in November 1985, Moran's appeal was
rejected. The Delaware Supreme Court concluded that in
adopting the rights plan the directors had fulfilled the business judgment rule, because Household's process had been
informed and deliberate. Before the August 14 board meeting
the directors were given notebooks containing a summary of
the plan; the essentials were provided at the meeting, along
with well-prepared legal and financial advice; Moran's opposition to the plan provided an informed critique; and there
was no evidence that the action was taken to entrench management.

In determining whether the plan was consistent with the
best interests of the corporation and its shareholders, the court's
criterion was whether the defensive mechanism was "reasonable in relation to the threat posed." The record reflected real
concern on the part of the directors over the increasing fre-
quency of bootstrap and bust-up takeovers in the financial
services industry. Household's board was on notice of Moran's
interest on behalf of DKM. The directors thus reasonably believed that Household was vulnerable to coercive acquisition
techniques. Hence, adoption of the rights plan had a "rational
corporate purpose."

By mid-1988 more than five hundred corporations had
adopted poison pills, most of them in reliance on *Moran* v.
Household International. In Donald Clark's words, "I paid a
price . . . but we made the point. . . . The plan does what
we said it would do and it doesn't prevent takeovers."

Poison pills do make the directors specially accountable in
a takeover situation. A board can cancel a poison pill at neg-
ligible cost. When a takeover proposal is presented to a corporation with a poison pill, the directors must decide whether

to remove an obstacle to the offer that only they can remove. The power to redeem the pill puts the board in the center of a takeover contest.

Adopting a pill, however, has potential disadvantages as well: It may increase the risk that outsiders will resort to proxy contests; alienate institutional investors; and expose directors to greater accountability by giving them greater authority. Also, rights plans are not perfect defenses; if they were, it is unlikely the courts would uphold them. Indeed, the stronger the pill, the greater the risk the courts will invalidate it. As someone said, "You can be a bull or a bear but you can't be a pig."

In deciding how rigorous a defensive system should be, a board's primary constituency today is likely to be the institutional investors, who respond negatively to the pill. In 1965 pension funds held only 6 percent of all corporate equity. In 1987 they owned about 25 percent. The Federal Reserve Board estimates that by the year 2000 that proportion could be 50 percent. And that figure does not include other institutions — mutual funds, insurance companies, banks, brokers, and dealers. In 1985, for the first time, more than half the shares that changed hands on the New York Stock Exchange were traded by institutional investors. The small investor has not disappeared, but most of his money is now in mutual funds. About eight million investors owned mutual funds in 1978; by 1985, that number more than doubled. In the same period the funds so invested rose from less than $7 billion to about $89 billion. These funds represent institutional investors as well.

Institutional investors used not to be active traders and almost invariably voted with management in proxy contests. No more. Institutional portfolios are managed by professional managers whose own short-term performance is continuously on the line. They are prepared to sell immediately and to trade often, and they want freedom to do so. Accordingly, many institutional investors — like the California Public Employees Retirement System and Teachers Insurance and Annuity Association — generally oppose defensive devices. In 1986, the

Council of Institutional Investors, representing thirty-one public pension funds with assets of $160 billion, disapproved poison pills. In 1987, it led fights against antitakeover provisions in forty shareholder meetings, including those of United Technologies, Control Data, and J. C. Penney; these fights were all lost. Many institutional managers routinely vote against staggered boards and fair-price provisions. Poison pills are not their kind of medicine.

PART II

o   o   o

FINANCIAL RESTRUCTURING: The Boardroom Response

o   o   o

Sauce for the Goose:
The Exclusionary
Self-tender

WALL STREET believes that a high stock price, more than any defensive maneuver, is the best protection against a takeover. If a company's share price is high, then it is less likely to attract a raider looking to buy an asset-rich company at a bargain. Fred L. Hartley, the sixty-eight-year-old chairman of Los Angeles–based Unocal Corporation, was credited with keeping his company's long-term debt burden low, but he was criticized for rejecting advice to raise the value of Unocal's stock through some form of financial restructuring. Ultimately, Unocal's low debt and low dividends made the company a target for T. Boone Pickens, Jr., and his group, Mesa Petroleum.

T. (for Thomas) Boone Pickens was known as the "terror of the oil patch" for his takeover attacks on such oil giants as Gulf Corporation, Phillips Petroleum Company, and City Service Company. The dramatic escalation of oil prices from $4 per barrel in 1971 to almost $40 in 1980 had made the stock price of oil companies cheap compared with the value of their oil in the ground. Pickens's takeover attempts resulted in either the acquisition of the target by another entity or in the target buying off Pickens at a premium not paid to other shareholders, commonly known as greenmailing. The payoffs gave Pickens hundreds of millions of dollars in profits and left the targets with staggering debt.

In April 1985, Pickens moved in on Unocal Corporation, formerly Union Oil Company of California. Mesa, already holding 13.6 percent of Unocal's stock, began a cash tender offer for 37 percent more. Mesa's offer had two tiers, designed to gain a bare majority of the Unocal shares in the first stage and then squeeze out the remaining shareholders at the back end through an exchange of Mesa securities. The securities to be issued in the squeeze-out would be high-risk, or "junk," bonds.

Junk bonds also can be sold by a target company to finance a defense against a raider, using proceeds from the sale to buy back its own stock and thereby compete with the raider in bidding to the company's stockholders. Many companies — learning from their attackers — responded to takeover threats by junk bond corporate restructuring or recapitalization.

One result of such defensive recapitalizations has been a significant increase in the leveraging of American industry. "Leveraging" means having debt along with equity as part of the company's long-term capital structure. When the business borrows money as part of its capital, it can increase the return to shareholders, but at the same time it increases their risk. The risk arises from the fact that the obligation to repay debt is fixed, while common equity has no fixed return and no repayment date. (The stockholders' interest in a corporation is called equity because originally their rights were protected not in the courts of law but in the separate courts of equity.) A stockholder gets returns only after the debt is taken care of.

The equity in the corporation provides financial cover for the debt, just as home ownership provides security for a home mortgage. With ample equity coverage, an investor putting his money in debt financing takes less risk than he does with an equity investment. Hence, the corporation generally can borrow at a lower rate of interest than the return it must pay to attract additional equity capital. In a conservative capital structure the debt/equity ratio may be 1 to 4. In a leveraged structure the debt/equity ratio may be as high as 9 to 1. There is less margin for business error in a leveraged situation, but raiders are prepared to run that risk.

Fred Hartley of Unocal was one of the longest-tenured, most powerful men in the oil industry and believed in keeping debt burden low and management authority clear. "This is a very tight organization," he said. "There is very little slippage as to who the heck is responsible." A newspaper story described Hartley as someone whom "Boone wasn't going to walk around like a chimpanzee." Hartley, a civil engineer by training, made Unocal a pioneer in premium gasoline, upscale highway truck stops, and prospecting for oil in deep waters.

In July 1965 Hartley had overseen what up to that time was the biggest corporate merger in history: Union Oil acquired Pure Oil in a friendly $900 million transaction that transformed Union from a regional West Coast company into the nation's twelfth-largest oil company, with sales of $11.5 billion a year and some twenty thousand employees. In a trial later arising from Mesa's takeover attempt, Hartley testified: "The purpose of the acquisition was to give the company greater geographic coverage domestically, internationally, and to broaden the base of the company so it was bigger and stronger to become a company of greater significance in the oil business in order that we could fully participate in the competitive arena in the areas of marketing, areas of getting our hands on government oil leases put up for auction . . . and to increase the earnings per share over a period of time."

Hartley was asked: "When you entered into . . . [this and] other acquisitions did you enter into them with an eye that the company would make money on its investment?" He replied, "No . . . we went out of our way to be sure we'd lose money. Good God. Of course, we made the acquisition to increase the quality of the company. That answers a damn stupid question."

The transaction between Pure Oil and Union Oil was an excellent example of a friendly merger, where two companies get together on a negotiated basis usually for synergistic purposes. These mergers require board approval of both companies, approval by the shareholders of the acquired company, and, in the case of stock transactions, sometimes approval by the shareholders of the acquiring company as well. However, in a friendly merger, by definition, the managements of both companies at least acquiesce and one of them strongly approves; otherwise there would be no deal for the directors to approve.

If management recommends the merger, has prepared the financial homework, and presents the case effectively to the board, a friendly merger is very likely to be approved. Management therefore normally controls a friendly merger. From the directors' viewpoint, such a merger proposal is like other board matters except that it is bigger in scale. If the merger is a mistake — and mistakes are sometimes made — that fact ordinarily will not be apparent to the directors. Management after all provides all the information upon which they base their decision: the financial projections, the plans for integration of operations, the legal and regulatory implications, et cetera. Indeed, the fact that a merger is a mistake ordinarily will not be felt for some time. There are exceptions, of course. Roger Smith of General Motors, the day after his first board meeting with Ross Perot as a member, may well have concluded that a mistake had been made. But this does not change the location of effective responsibility and control. Friendly mergers, whether or not they work out well operationally and financially, usually are management's call.

However, friendly mergers can be something less than friendly, as indicated in the jargon of mergers and acquisitions. There is a "bear hug," for example. A bear hug is a letter to the target communicating a fixed-price offer in terms that are firm, perhaps menacing. A "teddy-bear hug" may merely invite the target to negotiate without even mentioning price. An "iron maiden," on the other hand, contains a definite offer that is also publicized by the bidder. The publicity draws arbitrageurs and pressures the target's board to accept. If it is not accepted, such a bid may be followed by a tender offer to the shareholders. Indeed, even a "friendly" offer may be disclosed if it is fairly definite, and thus it can generate pressure from shareholders to negotiate a sale.

Tender offers appeal directly to the shareholders for control of the company, inviting them to tender their shares for sale at a specified price, either in cash or in securities of the offerer. An offer may be made for 100 percent of the target company's shares — "all" shares — or for "any and all shares," where the offer is not conditioned upon obtaining a minimum number of shares. Sometimes the offer is merely for enough shares to achieve control, typically 50.1 percent. An all-cash offer for all shares is the most attractive to shareholders and permits the offerer to wrest control quickly but usually involves a higher cost to the offerer. With the right strategy and under the right circumstances, the offerer can be in control on the twentieth business day after the offer is commenced.

Formally, a tender offer bypasses the board of the target company. If the board of the target has no objection to the offer, the offerer simply proceeds. Indeed, the company can facilitate the offer by making available its list of stockholders and simplifying the transaction's legal complexities. It can also recommend to the stockholders that they accept the offer, in effect making it a friendly tender offer. Whether a transaction will be friendly depends on the target board's evaluation of the price compared with what it believes might be obtained in the sale of the company.

An offer is called unfriendly because it fails to gain approval by the target company, not because it is necessarily disadvantageous to the company. In fact, a takeover could benefit the target company, by providing opportunity to replace its management, clean out "fat," redefine products, or exploit assets more efficiently. The unfriendliness lies in the fact that these good purposes — or the offerer's more direct purpose of simply making a profit — are proposed over objection of the incumbent management and board of directors.

In any case, a tender offer does not require management approval. For this reason it is a technique, along with a proxy contest or stock accumulation program, for carrying out a hostile takeover. Though the tender offer is made directly to the company shareholders, and the company's board cannot as such reject the offer, the board nevertheless can intrude. It can recommend to the shareholders that they not tender, or it can try to block the offer, for example, by challenging its legality in court, or by issuing a poison pill, or by junk bond corporate restructuring.

On the possibility of a friendly merger of Unocal into Mesa, Hartley was single-minded: no. "It is our strong desire, repeatedly affirmed by the board of directors, to continue to operate Unocal as an innovative, high technology company concentrating on long-term growth." In 1983, Unocal adopted a number of takeover defenses, including staggered terms for the company's directors and a fair-price provision. And Unocal was an active supporter of unsuccessful efforts to obtain federal legislation that would curtail takeovers by corporate raiders.

Congressman Timothy E. Wirth, a Colorado Democrat who chaired hearings about hostile corporate takeovers, summed up a position also taken by Hartley. "We see that the threat of corporate takeovers is the driving force behind major corporate decisions. How can we hope to compete internationally if major corporate activity in this country is driven by takeover threats, not by the desire to build better products for the long term? . . . [A]re corporate managers justified in taking steps to protect corporate assets from 'raiders' whose desire, we are told, is simply to turn a quick profit in the market at the expense of companies, employees, other shareholders and the economy long term? . . . In takeover battles, we see dramatic price and volume swings in the stocks of target and bidder companies. Small shareholders see the impact of large institutions and arbitrageurs moving in and out of the market, and believe they have insufficient information to compete with these market professionals."

Harrison J. Goldin, who as New York City comptroller was the manager of New York City pension funds exceeding $22 billion, presented a different view to the same subcommittee. "In the next century an American historian might devise the following summary of these hearings: 'Representatives of the entrenched executive suite defended their perks and sacred cow status against a band of raiders, sharks and greenmailers. Pension fund managers responsible for billions, whose dough it was in the mixing bowl, told a Congressional committee they liked neither the effort to secure greenmail nor the poison pill defense. They objected to shark repellents and sweeteners as additives, emphasizing that it was their dough being kneaded by others. They also said that if golden parachutes are to be given out as planes fall, there should be one for every passenger. . . . ' American corporate management is asking government help to quash . . . the initiatives of entrepreneurs seeking a quick buck in the marketplace, an instinct, after all, which has been a driving force of capitalism . . . we should resist governmental interference in this matter. . . . Takeovers are not inherently bad in themselves. Some are, adversely affecting a company's shareholders and the maximization of its assets through orderly long-term growth. But some are good, narrowing the disparity between a company's asset value and the market price of its stock." According to Goldin, "The issue . . . is basically this: when dealing with a public enterprise, whose company is it anyway? The answer? The shareholders'. It is their prerogative to make basic policy decisions about the direction of a corporation: whether it should or should not be sold; whether it should be taken over or not; whether its management should be retained or replaced. . . . Legislation to restrict mergers and acquisitions would effectively substitute the judgment of government for the judgment of shareholders as collective owners of companies. This would frustrate the free market. . . . In a word, should Mr. Pickens . . . or others care to hold an open auction for any of the stocks in our pension portfolios, I would not restrain them, nor would I want government to restrain them, either."

Federal legislation already regulates important aspects of tender offers. The Williams Act, enacted in 1968, is the basis of an SEC rule requiring that a purchaser file a form known as a Schedule 13D within ten days of acquiring 5 percent of a company's shares. The filing must be sent to the company and to stock exchanges and must indicate the purchaser's general plans for the target and whether the purchaser plans further acquisitions of the target's stock. On February 14, 1985, the Pickens-led partnership filed a 13D disclosing its purchase of 7.9 percent of Unocal's stock and stating that it was making only an investment and had "no present intention of seeking to obtain control." Unocal publicly complimented the Pickens group for making a "good investment." Privately, however, "we quit working on what we were working on," said Hartley, and "started working on the immediate problem." A five-member strategy committee was created, headed by Hartley.

One takeover strategy is simply to accumulate shares through purchases in the open market. This requires that there be stock available whose purchase would not materially move the market. In a friendly takeover, privately negotiated purchases can be arranged. In a hostile one, a "toehold," or "creeping," acquisition can be realized through carefully buying stock in the market — initially through secret accounts — until the 5 percent threshold is reached and during the ten-day period thereafter, prior to filing the 13D. This was the technique Pickens used in his initial move against Unocal.

The purchaser may try to buy control at market prices without paying an acquisition premium. Or he may seek something less than control as a base for a next move, such as a proxy contest or blocking a defensive merger. Alternatively, the purchaser may aim to stir interest in the target — put it "in play" — to induce others to make bids. The purchaser can then sell his holding to the new bidder or sell it back to the target at a premium: greenmail.

From a target's viewpoint, the toehold acquirer is a threat. He has influence on transactions requiring shareholder approval. The toehold may attract the attention of professional arbitrageurs and short-term speculators, putting the company into play at an inopportune time. A toehold of course may be motivated by traditional investment considerations. Pickens initially said this was his purpose with Unocal, and some people may have believed him.

In early March, Unocal retained Goldman, Sachs. In the words of Peter G. Sachs, a partner with expertise in the oil and gas area, they were to focus on "a potential contested solicitation of proxies by the Pickens group" for positions on the Unocal board of directors. There was also the possibility that Pickens could propose liquidating the company or "some form of assets spinoffs."

On March 27, Pickens bought another 6.7 million shares and by the end of March accumulated 23.7 million shares, 13.6 percent of the total outstanding. Mesa announced that Drexel Burnham Lambert, a securities firm specializing in takeovers, had $3 billion ready in financing commitments. Mesa also had a credit line of $925 million from commercial banks. "All of us were just shocked," said one Unocal adviser, "when Boone came up with that money."

o   o   o

Just over a week later, on April 8, Mesa made a front end–loaded offer of $54 per share cash for 64 million shares, approximately 37 percent of Unocal's outstanding stock. If successful the offer would give Mesa control of Unocal. The back-end offer for the remaining shares would involve securities purportedly worth $54 per share. Guiding Mesa was its veteran takeover team, including Joseph Flom of the Skadden, Arps law firm and financial advisers from Drexel Burnham. This was Pickens's fifth assault on a U.S. oil company in as many years, but he had never yet succeeded in capturing his quarry. In Unocal's case, Pickens now made it clear he wanted to gain control. "Our single purpose is to gain control of the company . . . then we'll decide what we're going to do about the company," he said.

Pickens's announcement was a full-page ad in the *New York Times*, which read:

Notice of Offer to Purchase for Cash up to 64,000,000 Shares of Common Stock of Unocal Corporation at $54 Net Per Share by Mesa Partners II and Mesa Eastern, Inc., a wholly owned subsidiary of Mesa Partners II. The purpose of the Offer is to acquire a number of Shares which, when added to the Shares presently owned by Mesa Partners II, will constitute a majority of the outstanding Shares . . . as a step in obtaining control of the Company and ultimately acquiring the entire equity interest of the Company. Mesa Partners II owns on the date hereof 23,700,000 Shares, representing approximately 13.6% of the outstanding Shares. If Purchaser purchases an aggregate of 64,000,000 Shares pursuant to the Offer, the Purchasers will together own 87,700,000 Shares, representing approximately 50.1% of the outstanding Shares. The Offer and the proration period will expire on May 3, 1985, at 12:00 midnight, New York City time, unless extended. Withdrawal rights will expire at 12:00 midnight, New York City time, on Friday, April 26, 1985. The Purchaser will purchase shares pursuant to the Offer if, and only if, on or prior to the expiration date, sufficient financing is obtained by the Purchasers to enable them to purchase the Shares. In addition, the Offer is conditioned upon, among other things, a minimum of 64,000,000 Shares being validly tendered and not withdrawn prior to the expiration of the Offer.

The price of Unocal's stock rose $1 per share to $49¾.

Hartley learned of Mesa's offer on his car radio on the way to work. He thought the offer was inadequate. He later testified, "My general knowledge of what . . . [Pickens's] appraisal was of our own company and . . . other prices that companies had been raped for seemed like a low number. . . . I have been in this company 46 years, and I have seen it grow from nothing to something, and seen my own shares multiply and multiply in value and giving me a price . . . $10 above market at the time the tender offer was made. . . . [T]o get an increase above market of about . . . 25 percent . . . was chicken feed."

A takeover bid is a business blitzkrieg requiring instant mobilization. The outsider will already have reconnoitered, decided whether to keep the company alive, and chosen who will run it. Responding to a takeover requires crisis management. Unocal's board had six inside and eight outside directors. All the inside directors were also members of the executive committee: Hartley; Claude S. Brinegar, senior vice president, administration; Ray A. Burke, senior vice president, energy resources; T. C. Henderson, senior vice president, and president of the Union Chemicals Division; William S. McConnor, senior vice president, and president of the Union 76 Division; and Richard J. Stegemeier, senior vice president, corporate development.

The board met on April 13 to consider the situation. No agenda or written materials had been provided. A detailed oral presentation was made by teams of financial advisers and lawyers: Peter Sachs of Goldman, Sachs, a firm that as a matter of policy refused to advise companies making hostile bids and that often advised companies receiving hostile bids; Dillon, Read, according to Hartley "spiritually committed to what I consider to be the American economic way"; lawyers from Sullivan & Cromwell of New York and Gibson, Dunn & Crutcher of Los Angeles; and Wilmer, Cutler & Pickering of Washington, D.C. Unocal's financial advisers regarded Mesa's offer as wholly inadequate; in Sachs's opinion, a minimum cash value was $60 per share, $6 above Mesa's offer. Sachs said a reasonable range was $70 to $75 a share.

One defensive strategy was a self-tender by Unocal — an offer by the company to buy its own stock from shareholders. At $70 to $75 per share a self-tender would require heavy borrowing, an estimated $6.1 billion to $6.5 billion of additional debt. Unocal could remain a viable entity but might have to reduce exploratory drilling or otherwise retrench operations. A second strategy would be a leveraged buyout by management and other private investors, to be financed mainly by borrowing against the company's assets. Liquidation — selling all the company's assets — was theoretically a third possibility. However, such a transaction would take sixty to ninety days and therefore could not be completed within the twenty-day tender offer deadline.

The eight outside directors then met separately with Unocal's financial advisers and attorneys. They agreed unanimously to advise the board to reject Mesa's tender offer and to pursue a self-tender. When the board reconvened, that decision was reiterated.

Unocal's self-tender offered its shareholders a price higher than the first stage of Pickens's two-tier offer and thus would discourage tenders to Mesa. At the same time, the payout would reduce the company's value to Mesa should Mesa's offer succeed. Retiring shares by buying them up also would reduce the "float" — shares held by shareholders readily willing to trade and thus most likely to accept a tender offer. And under Delaware law, shareholder approval was not required for a self-tender offer. Unocal hoped the self-tender would so dramatically change the company's financial condition that Mesa would terminate its offer.

On April 15, the board met once again, this time for two hours. Philip Blamey, Unocal's vice president of finance, presented the proposed self-tender offer. Hartley later testified, "The investment advisers told us they had appraised the value of the shares by all of the criteria used by investment bankers; other deals that are being made, for example, $80 a share paid by Chevron to Gulf, and any and all other deals. . . . They considered the record of the company and its ability to grow, and from whatever angles they came down on, they were quite satisfied that the shares were worth at least $72 a share. We kicked around numbers all the way up to $80 a share." The lower end of the range was $70 per share. "Our investment bankers said they would be comfortable with $72," Hartley commented. "That was their sage advice."

The directors agreed upon $72 in debt securities rather than cash. The board was advised that restrictions on the sale of corporate assets and limitations on corporate debt would have to be imposed until the obligations were paid. Moreover, the Unocal offer was to go into effect only if Pickens's tender offer was successful. Thus, if Mesa acquired 50.1 percent of the outstanding shares, Unocal would then buy the remaining 49 percent with its self-tender. That would preempt the second stage of Pickens's two-tier offer. Instead, Mesa would be confronted with senior debt greater than the value of its equity in Unocal. The Unocal offer was subject to one other important condition: Its offer did not extend to Mesa. Like certain forms of the poison pill, the Unocal offer gave to every stockholder except the raider a right to sell their stock back to the company.

Pickens denounced the measure as a "poison pill in a new bottle." Hartley, in a *Los Angeles Times* interview, said he did not like the defensive measure, but that in a "junk bond irresponsible society" he had no choice. He acknowledged that Unocal's self-tender would wipe out the company's net worth but said Unocal bonds were better value than Pickens's bonds. Unocal had been a growth company, adding around $500 million a year to its equity since 1980. Shareholders in such a company usually are willing to sacrifice dividend returns in favor of asset buildup. But, according to Hartley, "the financial mafia on Wall Street is a new force to deal with. . . . The battle today is not Hartley versus Pickens or Unocal versus Mesa. . . . Our economic system is at stake. Communism is all debt. There is hardly any equity left in South America . . . and now we're doing the same damn thing to ourselves."

To the press's question "How much stock do you own in Unocal?" Hartley replied: "I've got about 220,000 shares, and I've got another 60,000 shares in my profit sharing. . . . Pickens cannot accuse me of putting my money into Treasury bills and having no confidence in the company. That's just pure Picken-pulp." Pickens pretended no surprise at Unocal's exchange offer. After all, he said, "we didn't come to town on a load of watermelons."

On April 22, Unocal amended its plan, now offering to buy 50 million shares for $72 per share whether or not the Pickens offer was successful. When Hartley later was asked, "How comfortable were you with [Unocal's] commitment . . . to buy back 50 million of its shares . . . can you remember . . . saying that you are not entirely comfortable with the increase

in the debt, but that it did not put the company into a catastrophic arena?" Hartley replied: "Yes . . . as a result of our
$72 a share for 50 million shares, . . . we would spend [$]3.6
billion, and we would raise the company's debt load to about
[$]4.8 billion . . . which becomes a completely new ball game
for the operation of the company, but that we would be able
to live with it . . . I think the use of the terminology, I was
not entirely comfortable, is in the context of saying that putting debt into the company is not a happy thing to do for a
company that has a great, great historical record of spending
its cash flow to cause growth, to create jobs, to make America
a better country."

Unocal's legal counsel had advised that Mesa could be excluded from the offer only for a valid corporate purpose. The
directors focused on protecting shareholders at the back end
of Mesa's proposal. Unocal's 49 percent exchange offer, like
all tender offers that may be oversubscribed, contained a proration clause. This requires that if more shares were tendered
than covered by the offer, acceptances would be prorated
among those tendering their shares. If Mesa was allowed to
participate in the Unocal tender, under the proration provision every Mesa share accepted by Unocal would displace one
held by another stockholder. That would defeat the aim of
protecting shareholders who didn't sell in the first stage of
Mesa's offer. Moreover, if Mesa could participate, it would
thereby obtain financing for its own program.

The board had unanimously agreed that excluding Mesa
from the offer had been right. "A vote wasn't necessary," said
Hartley. "I have a technique in corporate democracy of going
around the room and asking the directors if they have any
further comments, anything to the contrary, and we get a
consensus that way."

At the same time that Unocal amended its offer, Pickens
filed suit in Delaware. On April 27, Hartley's deposition was
taken in Los Angeles. He was asked:

Q: — When did you first seriously consider a self-tender by
    Unocal for its shares, you personally? . . .

A: — Oh, I think we have talked about self-tendering for stock for years. That's known as buying back your shares. Many companies are doing that.

Q: — . . . I understand that the board gave the executive committee authority to purchase up to a hundred million dollars of its own shares within the last 18 months; is that correct?

A: — I can't affirm to you the 18 months, but it was some time ago.

Q: — And over that period the executive committee did not buy back any of its own shares?

A: — That is correct.

Q: — And if I recall some of your public remarks correctly, it was simply because the market price was wrong?

A: — No. The reason is that we are an operating company, not an investment company. When you start buying your own shares, you are sort of getting into an area of buying up stock, and that, of course, reduces the funds that you have available for investment — for operations of the company, capital investments, et cetera.

Q: — Now, the self-tender which was announced by the company on April 16 or April 17 will also result in a reduction of operating expenditures, will it not?

A: — Certainly.

Q: — Why did you change your mind?

A: — Because Mesa made a grossly undervalued bid for the company. With a lot of junk paper.

Q: — . . . What did your independent advisers tell the executive committee was the value of the assets of Unocal?

A: — They arrived at their evaluation in the way that independent financial advisers do, and that's their business, and it is not mine, and . . . I don't know all aspects of their evaluation techniques because I am not a financial adviser. . . .

Q: — Did the investment advisers on either April 13 or April 15 tell the board of directors what they believed the assets of Unocal were worth?

A: — Their conclusion was that the assets were quite sufficient to justify pricing the tender offer for Unocal stock
at $72 a share. . . .

Q: — Why did you as chairman and chief executive officer of
the company determine to distinguish between Mesa
and any other shareholder of the company?

A: — Because Mesa was making a raid on our company. . . .

Q: — Do you distinguish in your own mind how a long-term
shareholder should be treated as between those who are
perhaps not — those who seek to maximize their investment on a short-term basis?

A: — I think those shareholders of ours who are truly investors, whether they bought their stock recently or held
it for umpteen years, treat them all the same. That's
highly different than those shareholders who have announced they wish to take over the company and destroy it.

Judge Carolyn Berger, the Delaware trial judge, thought
otherwise. On April 29, she issued a temporary restraining
order prohibiting Unocal from proceeding unless Mesa was
included. A temporary restraining order is a very short-term
postponement, putting things on hold until the court can consider a preliminary injunction. A preliminary injunction is a
longer-term provisional order that puts things on hold until a
full trial can be held, and possibly an appeal. On May 13,
Judge Berger granted Mesa a preliminary injunction. Although the trial court recognized that directors could attempt
to defeat a hostile takeover that they considered adverse to
the best interests of the corporation and its shareholders, it
ruled that the transaction had to treat all shareholders
equally.

The trial court authorized Unocal to appeal to the Delaware
Supreme Court without waiting for a full trial. Because the
proration date under Unocal's offer was May 17, 1985, and
Mesa's tender offer expired on May 23, the appeal was expe-

dited to May 16. On May 17, the Delaware Supreme Court gave its decision orally.

o o o

Mesa had argued that the discriminatory exchange offer violated a fiduciary duty owed to all Unocal shareholders. It is a basic principle of corporate law that all holders of the same class of shares have the same rights and privileges. Dividends must be paid equally, and voting rights must be equal per share for each class of stock. Mesa contended all shareholders must be treated equally in a tender offer.

Unocal argued that the two-tier aspect of Mesa's tender offer itself was unequal toward Unocal shareholders other than Mesa. The Unocal exchange offer simply offset this inequality by neutralizing the coercive effect of Mesa's tactic on the other shareholders. Furthermore, the process followed by the Unocal board demonstrated that its action was made carefully, in good faith, and on an informed basis, and hence was protected by the business judgment rule.

The Delaware Supreme Court began by reviewing the authority of the board under the Delaware Corporation Law, Section 141(a). This provision speaks generally to the board's authority: "The business and affairs of every corporation organized under this chapter shall be managed by or under the direction of a board of directors, except as may be otherwise provided in this chapter or in its certificate of incorporation."

This "constitutive," or "empowering," rule is the foundation of corporate governance. Legal rules usually are thought of as prohibitions and penalties — speed limits, the income tax law, and legal liability for damages. However, another kind of rule authorizes people to take action or make policy. In the larger scheme of things, these constitutive rules are as important as prohibitions and penalties. For example, provisions in the United States Constitution authorize Congress to levy and collect taxes and to regulate interstate commerce. Under this legal authority Congress can modify the internal economic structure of the United States through taxes and regulation.

Similarly, the Constitution permits the president to fire cabinet officers. Section 141(a) of the Delaware Corporation Law gives a corporation's board of directors similar powers over the corporate entity.

In addition, the powers exercised by the Unocal board derived from Section 160(a) of the Delaware Corporation Law, which confers broad authority upon a corporation to deal in its own stock. "Every corporation may purchase, redeem, receive, take or otherwise acquire, own and hold, . . . lend, exchange, transfer or otherwise dispose of, pledge, . . . and otherwise deal in and with its own shares." On the basis of this section, a Delaware corporation may deal selectively with its stockholders in the acquisition of its shares, provided the directors have not acted out of a primary purpose to entrench themselves in office.

The board also has power derived from its duty to protect the corporate enterprise, including stockholders, from outside harm. The court observed that a board of directors "was not a passive instrumentality."

Generally speaking, in exercising their authority, the directors are protected by the business judgment rule. The business judgment rule is that a court will not substitute its judgment for that of the board if the board's decision is made in good faith and on an informed basis and has a "rational business purpose." In addressing a takeover bid, a board must determine whether the offer is in the best interests of the corporation and its shareholders. However, when a corporation purchases its shares to remove a threat, it has the effect of strengthening incumbent management's control. Accordingly, the directors confront an unavoidable conflict of interest. In the language of the courts, there is an "omnipresent specter that a board may be acting primarily in its own interests, rather than those of the corporation and its shareholders." The directors therefore have an "enhanced duty" to show reasonable grounds for their decision in a takeover situation. Such a showing is more easily made where a majority of the board consists of outside independent directors.

Speaking specifically to forestalling Pickens's takeover bid, the Delaware Supreme Court held that "a defensive measure to thwart or impede a takeover must indeed be motivated by a good faith concern for the welfare of the corporation and its stockholders, which in all circumstances must be free of any fraud or other misconduct." It must also be "reasonable in relation to the threat posed." This requires the directors to analyze such factors as the "inadequacy of the price offered, nature and timing of the offer, questions of illegality, the impact on constituencies other than shareholders, *i.e.,* creditors, customers, employees, and perhaps even the community generally, the risk of nonconsummation, and the quality of securities being offered in the exchange."

The court cited studies in 1979 and 1982 indicating that where a hostile takeover was defeated, the company's stock usually thereafter either traded at a higher price than the rejected offer or brought another takeover bid at a higher price. It noted that the threat "was posed by a corporate raider with a national reputation as a 'greenmailer.'" It observed that as the sophistication of raider techniques increased, increasingly sophisticated defensive measures had received judicial sanction, including "devices bearing some rather exotic, but apt, names: Crown Jewel, White Knight, Pac Man." Compared with these strategies, Unocal's exchange offer was reasonable. Moreover, said the court, "if the stockholders are displeased with the action of their elected representatives, the powers of corporate democracy are at their disposal to turn the board out." Accordingly, the Delaware Supreme Court reversed the trial court, vacating the preliminary injunction.

o o o

Immediately following the decision, Pickens and Hartley met to discuss settlement. A settlement was reached under which only 32.5 percent of Mesa's holdings would be purchased, as opposed to 38.4 percent of other shareholders' stock. Mesa also entered a twenty-five-year standstill agreement, agreeing to stay away from Unocal; to vote all its shares as Unocal directed; and to sell its remaining 16 million shares only under certain conditions. Pickens stood to lose $40 million to $80 million, depending on the future price of Unocal stock. He bought at an average price of $44.72; the shares closed on May 21 at $35.88. Some analysts called the result reverse greenmail.

Unocal remained an independent company but at a high price. It bought back 40 percent of its shares for $5.3 billion. To do so it incurred debt that brought its total debt load to $5.9 billion. Investment banker fees totaled $25 million, legal fees just under $10 million. As it happened, the company also immediately confronted falling oil prices. Unocal's stock, which had hit a high of $51 per share during the takeover battle, dropped to a low of $15.63 per share on July 3, 1986. Hartley refused to reduce debt by selling assets such as oil and gas reserves or its Union 76 gas stations. In Hartley's words, that would kill "the goose that lays the golden egg."

Reflecting upon the fate of Unocal, Hartley told the press, "We did the best we could in a society that's lost its morality and ethics. Our shareholders didn't get hurt, our employees' position was preserved, our ability to serve our customers continued and the company remained intact."

The courts give great deference to the board's judgment, as illustrated in *Unocal*. On the other hand, in evaluation of defensive tactics a new requirement appeared in that decision: The court must be satisfied that the board's action is "reasonable in relation to the threat posed." This requirement does not substitute the court's judgment for that of the board, but it is something more than requiring a certain process, because it goes to the reasonableness of the actual decision. What is "reasonable" inevitably means what a court will find to be reasonable.

A year after the Delaware Supreme Court found in favor of Unocal, in July 1986, the SEC amended the tender offer rules to prohibit exclusionary tender offers, the technique Unocal had used. All holders of the same class of stock must now have opportunity to participate on an equal basis. Although this federal regulation invalidates the specific technique used by Unocal, it does not undercut the legal principle developed in the *Unocal* case. The raider's proposal sets the ground rules for the game. If his proposal treats stockholders unequally, he may be subject to the same treatment. Sauce for the goose.

○   ○   ○

CHAPTER 4

Its Own White Knight

O N MONDAY, December 3, 1984, Warren M. Anderson, chairman of the board of Union Carbide, was told that there had been an accident at the company's plant in Bhopal, India, and that deaths had occurred. Anderson immediately left for India with a technical and medical team. On arrival at the Bhopal airport, he was arrested on charges of criminal conspiracy and negligence in the Bhopal gas leak. Demonstrators carried signs reading "Hang Anderson." Six hours later he was released on bail for 25,000 rupees (the equivalent of $2,000) on the condition that he leave the country to avoid stirring up "strong passions." As he left, American lawyers for plaintiffs arrived to solicit what came to be thousands of lawsuits against Union Carbide. A $15 billion class action suit was filed in West Virginia by Melvin Belli of San Francisco. Anderson later described the lawsuits as an involuntary takeover defense, "the ultimate poison pill."

In June 1985, GAF, a New Jersey chemical and building material company a tenth of Carbide's size, began open market purchase of Carbide common stock. GAF's chairman and CEO, Samuel J. Heyman, was a magna cum laude graduate of Yale University, a graduate of Harvard Law School, a former federal prosecutor, and a onetime real estate developer. Heyman saw the Bhopal disaster differently, based on experience with massive asbestos litigation in which GAF had been involved. Heyman concluded that Carbide could settle Bhopal comfortably, given its $200 million in insurance and close to $1 billion in pension fund surplus.

In 1983 Heyman had emerged from his family-owned shopping center business in Westport, Connecticut, to wage a proxy campaign against GAF's incumbent management, calling it a "textbook case of corporate mismanagement and ineptitude." Jesse Werner, the CEO of GAF, had taken charge in 1961, when the company was still controlled by the U.S. government, which had seized GAF as enemy property in 1942. Before that GAF had been General Aniline & Film Corporation, a division of the German I. G. Farben empire. GAF sales expanded rapidly in the 1970s, rising to more than $1.2 billion in 1979, but earnings thereafter lagged and then lapsed into losses.

"When the GAF thing got going," said Martin A. Siegel, director of mergers and acquisitions at Kidder, Peabody and a neighbor of Heyman's, "no one really took him for real. They didn't realize how very determined and very tenacious he was." But Heyman attracted strong support among institutional investors. At GAF's 1983 annual meeting, the Heyman Committee for New Management, although controlling less than 7 percent of GAF's shares, elected its nominees to the board with an estimated 7.4 million votes cast against 5.3 million for the management slate. Werner challenged the election in court but yielded power when his appeal was rejected late in the year.

Heyman took over as chairman and CEO and turned the company around. It realized a profit in 1984 and boosted profits by 44 percent in the first half of 1985. Heyman pumped money into GAF's chemical business and began looking around for another chemical company with high cash flow, shares trading at a discount from book value, highly centralized management, and excessive overhead. In Heyman's judgment, Union Carbide met all these criteria.

Union Carbide, a producer of industrial gases, petrochemicals, and consumer goods, was the nation's third-largest chemical supplier behind Du Pont and Dow, with seven hundred plants in more than thirty-six countries. Its 1984 sales were approximately $9.5 billion. Carbide's stock sold at $74 per share in 1982; in December 1984, just before Bhopal, it was selling at about $50; following the disaster it traded at $32.75. At that point, Union Carbide had been reducing its reliance on commodity chemicals and increasing emphasis on consumer products, particularly Glad trash bags, Prestone antifreeze, and Eveready batteries. It was regarded as highly community-sensitive and had one of the country's best safety records.

Carbide's chairman and CEO, Warren Anderson, was a Brooklyn-born chemist, the son of a Swedish immigrant carpenter; he had won football and academic scholarships to Colgate University and later obtained a law degree. In forty-one years with the company, Anderson worked his way up the ladder, becoming chairman in 1962. His community-mindedness was reflected in his leadership of the National Energy Foundation, funded by the big oil companies to educate schoolchildren about how to conserve energy.

On July 24, 1985, Carbide's board, fearing that the company's stock was being accumulated, began review of defensive measures. One proposal was to amend the company retirement plan to allow the board, if threatened with an "unfriendly change of control," to vest its pension fund surplus directly in the plan beneficiaries. Carbide's pension plan, like those of most corporations, is built up by regular contributions at a rate calculated to meet the pensions when they come due. If the contribution rate is based on a low assumed rate of interest, and interest rates then increase, the fund accumulates more than necessary to cover the pensions. The excess is called pension fund surplus. Legally, the excess can be left indefinitely in the fund, or it can be returned to the company as a refund. Or it could be forthwith permanently dedicated to the pension fund, "vesting" it in the plan participants. If returned to the company, the pension fund surplus is pure liquid capital. The proposal gave the board the power to vest the surplus and thus block such a return.

John Stichnoth, Carbide's general counsel, explained that "the proposed provision also will make it more difficult for a third party to rely upon the excess pension fund assets to finance, directly or indirectly, an unfriendly acquisition or change in control of the Corporation unless the board approves." According to Warren Anderson, "what we didn't want to do is leave those pension funds open for someone else who might not have the concern over the employees that we did. . . . [W]e have had through the past years . . . occasions where we have sold assets to other people. And as part of that asset sale, we have paid particular attention to what happens to those employees that go along with the business that we dispose of. . . . It's not just a dollar and cents arrangement. It's concern over employees, it's concern over a lot of things." The press called the amended plan a "pension parachute."

Carbide had strong outside directors, including John J. Creedon, president and CEO of Metropolitan Life Insurance Company; C. Peter McColough, chairman of the board of Xerox Corporation; and Harry Gray, chairman and CEO of United Technologies. Gray was also on the board of Citicorp and had experienced takeovers on both sides. Carbide's directors approved the amendment. They also amended the company bylaws so that special stockholders' meetings could be called only by management or the board. In addition, Carbide began a major restructuring to sell several unprofitable businesses and cut its salaried staff by 15 percent. The restructuring would yield cash that could be used to fight a takeover.

The day after Carbide's July 24 meeting, Heyman called to say that GAF had taken "an investment position" in the company's shares and to request a meeting with Anderson. A letter followed, repeating the message. Within three weeks, on August 14, GAF filed a Schedule 13D with the SEC stating that it had acquired nearly 4 million, or 5.6 percent, of the 70 million Union Carbide shares outstanding. A week later GAF reported its holdings had increased to 7.1 percent, and six days later to 9.9 percent.

Some Wall Street analysts tended to shrug off the Bhopal

disaster and, like Heyman, saw real value in the company, whose shares were trading at $50 just before GAF's August 14 filing. One estimated Carbide's worth at $95 per share on a breakup basis: book value of $70 per share, $14 per share in inventory values not shown on the balance sheet, and $11 in surplus pension assets. But could anyone realize those values? Carbide had reported earnings of $4.59 per share for 1984, less than a 7 percent return on equity and far below the approximately 12 percent return of the chemical industry as a whole.

On August 29, Heyman informed Alec Flamm, Carbide's president, that GAF was seeking approval to purchase up to 15 percent of Carbide's stock. This notification was required by the Hart-Scott-Rodino Act. The act requires filing information with either the Department of Justice or the Federal Trade Commission, followed by a thirty-day waiting period before purchases of a company's stock may exceed specified levels, a procedure that allows the enforcement agencies to block a takeover that they believe will violate the antitrust laws. The delay also gives a target more time to mobilize.

On September 10, Heyman and James T. Sherwin, GAF's vice chairman and chief administrative officer, met with Anderson and Flamm at Carbide headquarters, supposedly to work out a peaceful accommodation. A meeting between management and representatives of a hostile bidder can be a mistake, however. The bidder may infer that his maneuver is welcome or that the target management is afraid. It may result in market rumors and thus increase trading by speculators. Heyman's meeting with Anderson did indeed result in misunderstanding.

Anderson later testified that "I met with Mr. Heyman once . . . at that meeting [he] stated a number of things. He was familiar with our restructuring program, thought it made sense. . . . He said he was holding our shares for investment purposes. He had no suggestions to make that might augment our plan or program and it was a very amicable meeting. Next time I get a notice from Mr. Heyman to meet

I got a gun to my head." Heyman testified that he had mentioned a possible takeover.

The *Wall Street Journal* suggested that strong antitakeover measures would depress Carbide's stock and help Heyman in a proxy fight. But if Carbide did nothing, it might invite a tender offer. At this point, Carbide was also under enormous time pressure. Once the thirty-day Hart-Scott-Rodino period was over, Heyman could resume buying stock. Within twenty days thereafter Carbide could find GAF owning 20 or 25 percent of Carbide's stock, which would put Carbide in a very unstable position.

Carbide turned to Morgan Stanley, its investment bankers, and hired Sullivan & Cromwell as outside legal counsel. Would a drastic takeover defense be held to be in the best interests of shareholders or simply an effort to save top executive jobs? What was the threshold for judicial second-guessing?

Carbide's directors also had an insurance problem. The litigation in *Smith* v. *Van Gorkom* resulted in personal damages liability for the directors. This risk can be covered by "D & O" — directors' and officers' — insurance against liability for breach of the duty of care. However, by 1985 many insurance companies were refusing to write D & O insurance or would write it only at prohibitively high premiums. Carbide had lost practically all of its D & O insurance as a result of the Bhopal disaster. If found guilty of breach of duty to their shareholders, the Carbide directors therefore could be held personally liable for large damages.

Another way of protecting directors is for the company itself to provide indemnification, an agreement to pay any liability that the director incurs. But the corporation can do so only if it has sufficient assets, and, if the corporation is taken over by a hostile outsider, the successor management may be unwilling to do so. Moreover, indemnification is not allowed when a director is judged to have acted in bad faith.

Carbide's board considered but rejected a poison pill, out of concern that there would be charges of management entrenchment. Said Neil Anderson, the Sullivan & Cromwell partner who was to advise the board throughout, "The board felt very strongly about this." That left open only limited alternatives.

Anderson had created a takeover task force consisting of himself, three other members of management including Alec Flamm, and outside directors Harry Gray, chairman of United Technologies; Peter McColough, Xerox's chairman; and William Sneath, Carbide's retired chairman. In the words of Gray, the task force "considered the various alternatives which it might . . . recommend to a board in case of continued buying, in the case of an unfriendly tender offer. We did some look-sees at . . . parts of the company and it came out pretty evident that the thing you could do best with was with consumer products. . . . We aren't going to let Heyman take this company and break it apart. We can do it ourselves and get the value out to the stockholders and control the destiny of the people."

On December 10, GAF announced a partial tender offer at $68 per share in cash, seeking 48 million Union Carbide shares. According to Gray, "the very first that . . . we knew about it was a telephone call . . . because the newspapers got it, the offer really became public on the 9th, but officially it appeared as an advertisement in the newspapers on the 10th." Since GAF already held 7 million shares of Carbide stock, the tender offer would give it 80 percent of Union Carbide's outstanding shares. A merger would follow in which the remaining Union Carbide shares would be exchanged at approximately the same price.

The offer was subject to two conditions: that GAF obtain necessary financing, and that it receive a minimum of 31 million shares. GAF planned to obtain financing by issuing $2.35 billion in bonds and borrowing $1.5 billion more. The bonds would be paid off by selling Carbide's assets, particularly the consumer division, which produced Eveready batteries and Glad trash bags. Carbide thereby would be concentrated in the specialty chemicals and plastics businesses related to GAF's products. "By gaining control of Union Carbide," Warren Anderson later testified, "Heyman would hold to himself the chemicals and plastics business and the industrial gas business, which in fact would be had for nothing. And I felt that that was an unfair bust up program."

Arthur Liman of Paul, Weiss, Rifkind, Wharton & Garrison, here representing GAF, asked Anderson at trial, "I understand, Mr. Anderson, that you care very much about Union Carbide. I say that sincerely — "

A: — Does it show through?

Q: — It certainly does. You have been with it your whole career. And do you believe that company ought to be preserved as a whole?

A: — No, I think that any corporation is a living kind of endeavor, and you do change from time to time. We have done it ourselves. . . . I don't say you keep it intact. But wholesale bust-up-break-up doesn't make any sense to me.

Carbide had few options. The company already was $2.3 billion in debt and had uncertain but probably large Bhopal liabilities. Arranging a buyout or finding a white knight could prove difficult. Said Harry Gray, "The only one who could have served as a white knight . . . would have been me and I wouldn't have been able to sell the board of United Technologies, even though there was no competition, I couldn't have sold them on the returns of the capital."

Carbide's board met on Friday, December 13. Eric Gleacher of Morgan Stanley presented a financial analysis of the GAF offer, of each segment of Carbide's business, and of what might be realized in a liquidation. The calculations indicated that GAF's price of $68 per share cash, even without its financing contingencies, was unfair to Carbide's shareholders. "Morgan Stanley took us through a theoretical liquidation," Harry Gray later testified, "how long it would take for an orderly processing of liquidations, combinations, all types of avenues of maximizing the shareholder value. They then also had some analyses of . . . world economics, their assessment of the chemical industries, its turnaround . . . all these things were inter-

preted in the form of balance sheets, as well as operating
statements, and the bottom line, what expected earnings could
be. In each case . . . it gave a range, it didn't say a precise
number. . . . But it was done so that prudent individuals
understanding business would be able to come to an understanding of the potential valuation or range of values.

"It seems to me it was as many as seven alternatives," Gray
continued, "one of which was a leveraged buyout. That was
thoroughly detailed. Another was . . . buying of our own shares
. . . looking for a white knight . . . the purchase by Union
Carbide of GAF. . . .

"Then," according to Gray, "Sullivan & Cromwell advised
us on the legal implications. . . . They went through a very
thorough analysis of the business judgment rule."

Q: — Did the board take any decisions at this meeting? . . .

A: — No. Morgan Stanley had prepared two rather volumi-
     nous studies, one was a base study and the other was
     all of the backup data from their study of other compa-
     nies in the chemical industry, or other comparable peer
     companies, and we as a board elected to take the ma-
     terial with us Friday, study it Friday night, study it on
     Saturday, so there was plenty of time for deliberation in
     our minds, and come back and reconsider on Sunday.

Q: — Did you take the materials home?

A: — I did.

Q: — And did you study them?

A: — I did.

The board reconvened Sunday morning in a meeting that
lasted until 3:30 P.M. Carbide's worth was estimated to be at
least $85 per share as an operating company or $100 a share
if Carbide's assets were liquidated. The board noted that GAF
had only $150 million in financing commitments, which meant
that additional financing might be on such unfavorable terms
that GAF would later have to conduct a fire sale of Carbide's
assets. The prospect of a poor price was reflected in the $68
GAF offer. A distress sale would also adversely affect Car-

bide's employees, creditors, customers, and suppliers, as well as the communities where the company operated.

Harry Gray testified that "after that . . . [Warren Anderson and other] inside directors excused themselves, and the advisors, Sullivan & Cromwell and Morgan Stanley, stayed with just the outside directors of the board and we cross-examined them. And again we went through summaries of both Morgan Stanley's position and Sullivan & Cromwell's position. Then the [inside] directors rejoined us and then a board vote was taken, . . . we unanimously . . . rejected the GAF offer."

The board concluded that the best alternative for the shareholders was a stock buy-back of Carbide's own shares. Under this plan, Carbide offered to purchase its shares for a package with an expected value of $85 per share, $20 in cash and the rest in debt securities. The offer did not exclude GAF and was open until December 31. Heyman would then have three options — he could raise GAF's bid of $68 per share, sell GAF's 10 percent Carbide stake into Carbide's stock buy-back, or leave his offer to shareholders on the table.

As reported in the *Wall Street Journal,* Carbide's strategy was primarily created by Gray, "the most important and calming member of Carbide's board." At trial Gray stated: "The board's deliberation was that if we are going to end up with, in effect, what is a leveraged buyout, why not do a leveraged buyout ourselves and let our own shareowners, Union Carbide shareowners, benefit from it, and let the cash and the notes flow through to them. And so what we have done is turned the shareowners into debt security owners. We would rather have them as owners, but if there's no alternative, we would rather see them have it than see some other organization benefit from the work the Carbide organization has done." Union Carbide may have been the first takeover battle in which independent outside directors took control of the defense.

The debt securities in Carbide's offer also had covenants restricting subsequent sale of Carbide assets. According to Anderson's testimony: "We put the bonds out and . . . put covenants in there so you can't sneak assets out from under those covenants."

Q: — That is one purpose. What is the other one?

A: — Deter GAF.

Q: — There is a reference to . . . [a] part of the prospectus and it says, "Such convenants might also deter other persons from attempting, through tender or exchange offers or by any means, to acquire control of the company, especially persons who would seek to finance such an acquisition by utilizing the company's own assets and borrowing capacity," correct?

A: — Correct.

Q: — And you regarded that as desirable, right?

A: — Yes.

Q: — Is it a fact, sir, that you are using the assets of Union Carbide to back your exchange offer?

A: — Yes.

Q: — Did you regard it as more appropriate for the management to be able to utilize those assets and credit in order to make its own offer than for a third person to be able to ultimately be able to have access to those assets in order to make its offer?

A: — This was aimed specifically, as the covenant said, against these bootstrap efforts and bust-up junk bonds as liens on the assets of Union Carbide to serve their own particular purposes.

Q: — And it was aimed against them even if the offer to your shareholders was all cash, right?

A: — What does all cash have to do with it? It's the value that concerns me.

Covenants in the Carbide plan limited the company's aggregate debt to $3.1 billion, the amount necessary to consummate an exchange for 70 percent of the outstanding shares. The debt securities thus were backed by Union Carbide's assets and cash flow and hence would trade at their stated value and be of investment-grade quality. About 50 percent of Carbide's stock was held by larger institutional investors. When the exchange offer began, institutional money managers, seeing a chance to make a quick profit, raised their stake in Carbide to more than 70 percent. Institutional investors, Anderson said, are "quarter-to-quarter shareholders interested only in instant gratification."

The board also decided to sell Carbide's consumer products businesses, its crown jewels, and distribute the proceeds to shareholders. A five-year effort to diversify into consumer goods and specialty chemicals was reversed. The decision troubled Anderson. "I don't think it makes a lot of sense," he said, "because those businesses cushioned Carbide's chemical business through down cycles, but if anybody's going to do it, we're going to make sure that the value goes to our share-holders, not GAF's."

On December 26, Heyman had responded by raising GAF's offer to $74 per share in cash. He also filed suit.

The suit, brought in federal court in Manhattan, posed this issue: Could the board of a New York business corporation, without amending its charter, issue corporate bonds whose credit value was protected by restricting the sale of the company's assets?

The trial judge, Milton Pollack, rejected GAF's claim, holding that Carbide's defensive actions were within the wide latitude of management authority, based on the informed, reasonable judgment of an independent board having no personal interests at stake.

Concerning the restrictive covenants, the court pointed out that securities are not in one standard form but are "as varied as are the imaginations of those who market them." Formulating the terms of a security takes account of the company's need for funds, cash flow, long-term growth plans, and the current investment market. Courts therefore should be "very circumspect" in declaring any particular method of raising capital to be improper. If there was reasonable business justification, evaluated according to the company's particular situation, it would be irrelevant that the plan blocked a tender offerer's strategy, even if that effect had been intended. The board's assumption that the covenants would give the bonds an investment-grade rating had been vindicated on December 23, when Moody's rated them BAA3.

GAF's expert testimony disintegrated on cross-examination. When asked if the Carbide restrictive covenants were similar to those in bonds put on the market by his own banking firm, GAF's expert acknowledged that they were. When asked whether the language came from the same legal-form book, the witness answered that "it does appear the language is generally similar." Heyman's cross-examination testimony was:

Q: — So the covenants that we heard about in the course of the last day [that] restrict asset sales don't prevent you from making your offer, is that correct?

A: — It does not legally prevent us, if we wanted to continue with a very highly leveraged company.

The court found that Carbide's bonds "essentially followed a pattern developed by the takeover bar, depending upon which side of the fence it was called to serve."

The court also sustained the so-called pension parachute, allowing the board to vest the pension fund surplus for the benefit of participating and retired employees in the event of an "unfriendly change of control." The court said: "Labor, at whatever level, should not be victimized. . . . These legitimate concerns . . . need not be left to the goodwill of an unfriendly acquirer of corporate control in the jungle warfare involving attempted takeovers." GAF's motion for a preliminary injunction was denied.

Faced with having to raise his bid to the $80 range and hence to pay nearly $6 billion for Carbide, Heyman withdrew. GAF kept its 10 percent stake in Carbide, remaining the largest shareholder and making realizable gains of $200 million. GAF's investment bankers and lawyers were paid approximately $60 million; Carbide's commercial bankers took in at least $14 million. "Wall Street," Warren Anderson commented, "is becoming a casino rather than an investment organization."

"Some of our best companies still look like chips on a gaming table," said Robert Kennedy in a speech delivered fifteen months later to the Conference Board. In April 1986, Kennedy, former president of Union Carbide's Chemicals and Plastics Group, succeeded Anderson as CEO. By then, Carbide's major restructuring was over. "We had to go deep in debt, buy back a lot of equity, and sell our battery products and home and automotive consumer businesses." Carbide had just sold the battery business for $1.4 billion to Ralston Purina and had sold other assets totaling $3.5 billion in previous months.

In 1987, following its restructuring, Carbide was still a $6.8 billion corporation. After selling at less than book value for most of the preceding ten years, the company now was selling for three times book value. According to Kennedy, in strategic planning "value matters most, and that value is not a reflection of size but of earnings quality . . . survival and growth depend . . . on how hard those assets are working to add shareholder value." Though Kennedy deplored "the cashing in of equity in American industry with debt that can cripple our ability to grow . . . there's a sense in which the company that finds itself a takeover target may have been asking for it." If the full value of a company is reflected in its share price, the company is reasonably safe. If it is not, the company, in Kennedy's words, "might be shark bait, as we learned the hard way at Union Carbide."

o   o   o

Gelco Corporation would also become a changed entity as a result of a self-tender and restructuring in the face of an aggressive raider. As with Union Carbide, Gelco's stock price was low in relation to its breakup value.

The company was founded by "Bud" Grossman, who built a family-owned Chevrolet dealership in Minneapolis into a major leasing and management services company. He also made millions on the side in an oil and gas exploration firm. Grossman held board seats on important regional companies, including Northwest Corporation, General Mills, Northern States Power, and Toro. Approximately 17 percent of Gelco's outstanding shares was held by the Grossman family, including Bud, his brother Harold, and Bud's son Andrew, all of whom were directors.

Gelco revenues and profits grew steadily until fiscal 1983, when the company lost $34.4 million, compared with profits of $36.7 million a year earlier. The losses arose mostly in CTI International Inc., a marine container company Gelco had acquired in 1980, and in Gelco's air courier business. Like other equipment lessors, Gelco was highly leveraged. By early 1986, deregulation, overcapacity, and shifts in the national economy forced down the price of the company's stock. The press forecast a takeover; Gelco began evaluating defensive strategies.

In early May 1986, Gelco's board adopted a poison pill in which one preferred stock purchase right would be issued for each outstanding share of common stock. Before the meeting, three volumes of materials had been furnished by the corporation's outside legal counsel, Fried, Frank, Harris, Shriver & Jacobson, and another volume by Drexel Burnham. Using slides, counsel explained in detail how the plan would work.

The pill was a right to acquire participating preferred stock at $63. It would be exercisable upon either an announcement that without the board's prior consent an outsider had acquired 20 percent of the voting power in Gelco, or an announcement of a tender or exchange offer for 20 percent of the outstanding common stock. The rights could be redeemed by Gelco's board on several conditions, including a merger with a friendly company. In addition, if a third party acquired 25 percent of Gelco's stock without board approval, a flip-in would activate. All shareholders other than the raider would then have the right to buy $126 worth of Gelco stock for $63. There was also a flip-over feature, under which Gelco's shareholders would have the right to buy the raider's shares at a discount.

The plan was approved by Gelco's directors only after lengthy presentations by Drexel Burnham as well as Fried, Frank. A shareholder vote was not required.

At the time Gelco was unaware of any specific acquisition threat. However, eight weeks later the board was advised that Unicorp Canada Corporation, headquartered in Toronto, had acquired 4.9 percent of Gelco's stock and was interested in increasing that holding to between 15 and 25 percent. Reacting to the threat, Gelco bought back Unicorp's stake at $19 per share, a $4.50 premium above market, in return for the Canadian firm's promise not to purchase Gelco shares for at least ten years.

In August, Gelco also adopted a restructuring plan worked out with Drexel and Merrill Lynch Capital Markets, the investment banking arm of Merrill Lynch. Four Gelco businesses were put up for sale, including the building and trailer services segment. A self-tender offer was prepared for up to 3 million shares of the company stock through a "Dutch auction": the prospective sellers could offer the number of shares and price they would take, which the company had the right but not the obligation to accept, with a range of $17 bottom and $20 top. In a Dutch auction, the company's objective is to buy the shares as cheaply as possible; the stockholders who desire to sell want to maximize the price. The amount Gelco would pay would be determined by the number of shares and the prices specified by tendering holders.

Financing for the self-tender was to be provided by selling 3 million shares of new preferred stock to Merrill Lynch at $20 per share. An additional 400,000 shares of the preferred stock could be transferred to Merrill Lynch at the same price. Investment bankers were becoming merchant bankers as well, both arranging corporate takeovers and buyouts and investing their own capital in them. The change, which had come about in the early eighties, was in response to Drexel Burnham, which provided financing for some of the massive takeovers (e.g., Unocal) by arranging for risk-oriented investors, the buyers of so-called junk bonds, to finance the bids. Investment bankers, such as Merrill Lynch Capital Markets, responded by furnishing their capital to fund buyouts or, as in Gelco, to provide short-term funds for defensive purposes. After putting in their own capital, later they would take themselves out by re-selling the junk securities to the public.

Significantly, the preferred shares had voting rights, the 3 million preferred representing an 18 percent voting position. Combined with Gelco's directors and management holdings, that block would constitute voting control. Though there was no limitation as to how the preferred shares would be voted, Merrill Lynch did agree to standstill conditions — it would not purchase any additional Gelco voting securities for thirty months except from Gelco, and resale of the preferred was restricted.

Gelco could redeem the preferred stock for the original price of $20 per share, plus accrued dividends. The proceeds from selling Gelco's businesses would be used in part to buy back the preferred shares sold to Merrill Lynch. In effect, the transaction was "bridge financing" for Gelco's self-tender.

The self-tender began on August 29, when Gelco's common stock was trading at $14.88 per share. The tender deadline was September 26. Coniston Partners, known for acquiring stakes in companies perceived as vulnerable to takeover threats, began buying Gelco shares in the open market. In the words of Gus Oliver, a former merger lawyer at Skadden, Arps who joined Coniston in 1984, "We're really buying a company's underlying assets at a discount to their market value. . . . The spread between our cost and the underlying value is our protection as well as our potential reward."

By September 25 Coniston had acquired 17.6 percent. On that same day Coniston offered Gelco a negotiated merger at $22.50 cash per share, conditioned on Gelco's rescinding the self-tender and the proposed preferred stock sale to Merrill Lynch. Gelco's shares rose $1.13 to $18.50.

In early October Gelco's board held a nine-hour meeting to consider Coniston's proposal. Merrill Lynch advised that Gelco's breakup value was between $31 and $34 but forecast that, with the restructuring, the value would reach $57.20 per share within four years. The board unanimously rejected the Con-

iston offer as inadequate. Gelco, after all, was simply proposing to buy its own stock, which would redound to its shareholders' benefit.

When, as a result of Coniston's offer, Gelco's stock rose to
$23 per share, the board canceled the pending $17–$20 Dutch
auction self-tender without having purchased any shares. The
directors also reauthorized selling the preferred stock to Merrill Lynch after obtaining an opinion from Drexel Burnham
that the sale was fair. Merrill Lynch purchased 3 million preferred shares at $20 per share, giving Gelco proceeds to buy
back common stock.

Gelco announced a new exchange offer for that purpose. It
would purchase up to 6 million shares of stock, $10 per share
in cash plus a receipt for one tenth of a share of preferred
stock having a liquidation preference — the amount that would
be paid on a liquidation of the company — of between $16
and $20. The structure of the offer encouraged all sharehold-
ers to tender at the low end of the liquidation preference. If
Gelco's exchange offer went forward and Merrill Lynch exercised voting rights over its preferred shares, Gelco directors
and management together with Merrill Lynch would control
53 percent of the company's voting power.

That day Gelco common closed at $23.75, up $1.25. Coniston now had a 17.5 percent block on which it could realize
a profit of about $17.4 million. On October 24, Coniston
nevertheless sweetened its bid to $26 cash for all of Gelco's
outstanding shares, about $338.1 million. Gelco rejected the
offer. Partly out of reliance on the Merrill Lynch financial
analysis and partly on the basis of its belief in the long-term
value of the company, the board concluded that Coniston's
offer was inadequate. Merrill Lynch exercised its option on
the 400,000 shares of preferred. Keith Gollust of Coniston told
the *Wall Street Journal:* "We offered $26 cash for Gelco shares
while the directors offered only $10 cash plus the remainder
in preferred shares. Then they term our offer inadequate, when
theirs is clearly inadequate."

Coniston sued in federal court in Minneapolis, seeking to

enjoin Gelco from purchasing any shares under the October 7 exchange offer; from using the cash proceeds from selling Gelco preferred to Merrill Lynch; from giving effect to voting rights for the preferred issued to Merrill Lynch; and from implementing the preferred stock purchase rights plan. Gelco, Coniston argued, was illegally obstructing Coniston's $26 all-cash tender offer.

The trial court upheld Gelco. Judge Robert G. Renner considered significant the fact that Gelco adopted the rights plan four months before Coniston's initial purchase of Gelco stock; hence it was part of an ongoing corporate restructuring plan and not simply a reaction. Moreover, Gelco's poison pill was not inevitably coercive, because the directors would be subject to their fiduciary duty in deciding whether to redeem the rights as part of an acceptable outside bid.

The court also considered the consequences of an injunction. Although Coniston claimed that it would be irreparably harmed, the court said it was by no means clear that Coniston would be precluded from obtaining control. In addition, Coniston's loss of its bid would result primarily in a loss of prospective profit. If the injunction was granted, however, Gelco could be dismembered.

Coniston argued that the public interest was best served by allowing shareholders to make a "free and uncoerced" choice between the offers. The court questioned whether "it is truly in the public interest to allow Coniston's cash bid to force an auction of a company in the midst of a pre-existing restructuring plan to boost shareholders' stock value."

Minnesota law, like Delaware law, provides a strong presumption in favor of a board's business decision. The judge determined, however, that defensive strategies that affect stockholder interests are subject to "heightened judicial scrutiny" to assure that they are "reasonable in relation to the threat shown." This, of course, was the rule that had been laid down in the *Unocal* case.

The injunction was denied. In February 1987, the United

States Court of Appeals affirmed the lower court's decision. Meanwhile, Gelco completed the sale of Gelco Vehicle Leasing, Inc., Puerto Rico, for $27 million, its Canadian courier unit for approximately $54 million, and its United Kingdom leasing for approximately $25.3 million. It purchased 6 million shares of its common stock through the tender offer. Coniston tendered its 17.5 percent. On a prorated basis, however, Coniston still held a 12 percent stake in Gelco's 7 million shares outstanding.

Bud Grossman had a restructured and "independent" Gelco, but not for long. In October 1987, General Electric Credit Corporation, the same group that had shown interest in Trans Union in 1980, offered to buy Gelco's 7 million shares for $35 per share, or about $250 million. This time Gelco's board was negotiating with a friendly suitor. As part of the acquisition, the board approved redeeming the outstanding warrant dividends, the rights plan, at 5 cents. Bud Grossman and Gelco's directors had to be satisfied with the outcome of their vigorous battle against Coniston's $26 offer: the sale of their restructured company a year later at $35 to one of the world's leading financial service organizations in a friendly deal.

o o o

Both the Union Carbide and Gelco cases involved accountable directors confronting an aggressive raider. In both battles, outside directors played a major role in restructuring the corporation to enhance shareholder value.

Courts give special credence to outside directors because they stand apart from management and between a raider and the corporation's shareholders. The outside directors, typically individuals of stature and financial means, are not dependent on the company for their primary livelihood. The more impressive their credentials, the greater their authority. However, to sustain their decisions in takeover situations, outside directors must establish a record of careful deliberation of thoroughly developed alternatives. The record is the legal basis for their decisions under the business judgment rule.

Moreover, their decisions must be made in the medium of professional reports — managerial, financial, and legal. The process produces structure and discipline.

Competent people nevertheless may be unwilling to accept directorships from fear of damages liability. This deterrent frustrates a policy of having independent directors act as decision makers in matters of corporate grand strategy. In the end, the inability of corporations to attract qualified outside directors is to the detriment of shareholders.

Independent directors have greater exposure to personal liability than in the past as a result of withdrawal of liability insurance by insurers, the precedent in *Smith* v. *Van Gorkom*, and the extraordinary increase in litigation arising from takeovers. However, there is movement toward limiting the directors' risk. Legislation reducing or eliminating personal liability for breach of directors' fiduciary duty has been adopted in many states, including Delaware, Ohio, Pennsylvania, and several others. More liberal provision has been made for indemnification rights. In addition, the American Law Institute project, directed by the independent law reform organization whose recommendations often have wide acceptance, has suggested clarifications in the law that reduce directors' risk of personal liability. Although there are fears that these reforms could weaken directors' accountability to shareholders, the law appears to be moving very rapidly in that direction.

Union Carbide and Gelco are examples of a target board, under the leadership of its outside directors, saying to the company's shareholders, "We offer you a package of debt and your own restructured company that will be worth more than what the raider is offering you." In both cases, whatever the raider bid, the target's assets would be used to give its shareholders more. Leverage is king, and Carbide and Gelco became their own white knights. Restructuring remained in the hands of the target board.

PART III

o o o

THE BIDDING TRILOGY

CHAPTER 5

o   o   o

Leveling the Playing Field

THE RESTRUCTURING of Revlon was done by the raider Ronald Owen Perelman, who stripped away product lines of the company he acquired to focus on core businesses. Subsequent sales of company divisions provided capital that enabled Perelman to repeat this strategy, earning him the title "Wall Street Stripper" from *New York* magazine for "removing the outer layers and then emphasizing the most appealing parts." Revlon, Inc., was his most celebrated act.

Whether raider or target, buyer or seller, the question is, What is the right price? No one knows. Since control of corporations is not bought and sold in an everyday market like stocks, bonds, and commodities futures, there is no readily ascertainable market price. Pricing is therefore a matter of conjecture, or speculation. At any given time, under any given conditions, the right price is the price a buyer is willing to pay.

Pricing a company poses a special risk for the company's directors. Not only can directors be personally liable if they approve what a court later finds is a grossly inadequate price, but most directors are also concerned about being fair to their shareholders. The would-be buyer, on the other hand, wants to pay as little as necessary. This minimalist inclination may be reinforced by the buyer's relative ignorance as to the soundness of the prospective acquisition, quite like that of a buyer at a horse market. When the prospective buyer is a publicly held corporation, its directors — at least in theory —

may have to worry about their liability to their shareholders if the price they offer is too high. If the purchase is to be accomplished by a merger, with the price paid in shares of the acquirer's stock, the value of those shares may be another variable. Yet on any given occasion there may be another buyer who is willing to go higher, because the acquisition could provide it with a better corporate fit or greater tax advantages or what it regards simply as an opportune price.

One way to reach the right price when selling a company is through an open auction. For Revlon, the final pound of the gavel sounded in court.

Ronald Perelman, chairman of the board and chief executive officer of Pantry Pride, a supermarket chain based in Fort Lauderdale, had been looking for companies to take over. After earning a master's degree from the Wharton School of the University of Pennsylvania in 1966, Perelman had joined his father's Philadelphia metal-fabricating business, Belmont Industries. Twelve years later, at age thirty-five, he went out on his own. "It wasn't enough," he said. Aided by family money, Perelman acquired 40 percent of Cohen-Hatfield Industries, a jewelry distributor and retailer listed on the American Stock Exchange. In 1980, Cohen-Hatfield paid $45 million for MacAndrews & Forbes Company, a licorice extract and chocolate supplier. After turning the company around, Perelman took the MacAndrews & Forbes name and in 1984, with $90 million raised by Drexel Burnham, bought out the other shareholders and converted MacAndrews & Forbes into a private holding company for other acquisitions. Within a few short years, he built the company into a $750 million miniconglomerate through larger and larger deals, acquiring such businesses as Consolidated Cigars and Technicolor Inc. Perelman, colleagues said, was "pushy, demanding, impatient, a screamer seeking some sort of recognition and wanting to get someplace fast, but polite, too."

In June 1985, Perelman took control of Pantry Pride, formerly Food Fair Inc., by purchasing approximately 38 percent of the company's stock. A prospectus in connection with a securities offering stated his objectives: "Pantry Pride is actively seeking to dispose of substantially all of its assets and businesses and to acquire new assets and businesses." Perelman borrowed to the hilt on Pantry Pride's assets and then sold nearly all of its stores, keeping only a corporate shell. Pantry Pride was a much smaller company than Revlon, but Revlon's stock was cheap compared with the company's earning power and its worth if split up and sold in pieces.

Revlon was the creation of Charles H. Revson, his older brother Joseph, and the chemist Charles R. Lachman — the *l* in Revlon. The business was started on New York's West Side in the Depression year of 1932 on a $600 investment. Charles Revson himself sold the first bottle of nail enamel. By 1939 Revlon was a million-dollar-a-year nail polish company, second only to Avon Products in sales in the cosmetics industry, with a line of lipsticks sold under the marketing phrase "matching lips and fingertips." After World War II, while competitors pushed the girl-next-door image, Revlon's big advertising campaigns suggested the allure of the attractive mistress, with great success. Its market strategy was that nail enamel should match different outfits and occasions, and it introduced a new color every fall and spring. *Fire and Ice* and *Cherries in the Snow* sold at high prices; the enamel without the box and bottle cost almost nothing.

In early 1965, Revson bought U.S. Vitamin and Pharmaceutical Corporation for $66 million. Around that business, Revson built a health care division that took advantage of the rapid growth of national expenditures for medical services and supplies. By the late 1960s, Revlon was one of the three hundred largest corporations in the United States. The company lacked only a successor to Charles Revson, who by then was over sixty-five. Selection of Revson's successor as president and CEO became its central strategic concern. Revson forced out the first three successors that the board found for him. Said one, "It was impossible to work for him because you had no role." However, once Revson himself decided Revlon should have a president, he wanted the best. He considered John DeLorean of General Motors but decided on Michel C. Bergerac, a reserved, French-born former Fulbright scholar. Bergerac, then forty-two, head of ITT's extensive European operation, was a professional manager with experience in mergers and acquisitions.

Revson contacted Bergerac in Brussels and invited him to dinner on Bergerac's next trip to New York. In the course of the evening in Revson's apartment, Revson asked Bergerac if he could guess why the meeting had been arranged. Bergerac suggested, "You could be interested in selling your company for estate purposes; or you could want to hire me." Revson was incensed at the idea that he might want to sell Revlon. "This company will never be sold out to anyone! No one is going to take over Revlon, now or ever." Revson returned to his agenda. "It was an interesting romance," Bergerac admitted.

Upon being named Revlon's president in 1974, Michel Bergerac received a $1.5 million bonus, a five-year contract at $325,000 a year, and a stipulation that if he was not made CEO within a year he could resign and collect $1.3 million more. There were also options on 70,000 Revlon shares — all in all, in Bergerac's words, an "extremely attractive" offer.

A year later, Revson surrendered his position as chairman and CEO to Bergerac. With Revson's blessing, Bergerac immediately reorganized the company's operations, decentralizing what had been a one-man show. When Bergerac joined Revlon, the company's annual sales were less than $500 million. In ten years the figure stood at $2.5 billion, growth resulting for the most part from Bergerac's acquisitions in the thriving health care field: drugs, vision care, and medical diagnostics. By 1985 that field accounted for 66 percent of Revlon's operating profits. Companies "were bought at right prices," said Bergerac proudly, "and we built their values." He had changed Revlon into a health care company.

Although gross revenues had expanded tenfold in the health care division and fivefold in the company as a whole, after 1980 profits began to lag. Earnings peaked that year at $192.4 million, or $4.87 per share; by 1984, facing fierce competition and loss of market share in cosmetics, the company's earnings had fallen to $112 million, or $2.99 per share. At the end of July 1985, Revlon's shares were trading at $42.50; their total market value was $1.6 billion.

Perelman and Bergerac first met in mid-June 1985 at Bergerac's apartment, a meeting requested by Perelman. The meeting was arranged through Joseph Flom, a Skadden, Arps partner and counsel to Perelman and Pantry Pride, and Simon H. Rifkind, a director of Revlon. Perelman told Bergerac that Revlon was one of a number of companies with which Pantry Pride "had a possible interest in pursuing acquisition discussions" and that he understood "that Bergerac was interested in exploring the possibility of such an acquisition." Bergerac indicated that Perelman was correct, stating, however, that Revlon's board would approve only "a price which began with a 5." Perelman suggested a price in the range of $40 to $50 per share. Bergerac dismissed those figures and ended the discussion. Bergerac and Perelman were to have dinner the next week to continue discussions; on the scheduled day, however, Bergerac canceled. Subsequent overtures by Perelman were resisted, perhaps in part, as noted in the Delaware Supreme Court's opinion, because of Bergerac's "strong personal antipathy" to Perelman.

The door of a friendly takeover having thus been at least temporarily closed, on August 14, 1985, Perelman tried another. Pantry Pride's board authorized him to acquire Revlon, either through negotiation in the $42–$43 per share range or by making a hostile tender offer at $45.

Perelman urgently requested a meeting with Bergerac to discuss a proposal. At a meeting held at the office of Arthur Liman, a partner at Paul, Weiss, Rifkind, Wharton & Garrison, Revlon's regular outside counsel, Perelman presented Pantry Pride's offer. Bergerac replied that he was not prepared to have discussions under threat and immediately decided to retain Wachtell, Lipton as special counsel to develop strategy for dealing with Pantry Pride.

In fact, there was some effort to reach a friendly deal. Several of the key participants had common acquaintances: Simon Rifkind, on Revlon's board, was also on the board of Perelman's holding company, MacAndrews & Forbes. However, because he was a director of both parties, at some point he would have to withdraw from the deliberations and perhaps resign from at least one of the boards. When Perelman refused to abandon his takeover threat, Rifkind resigned as a director of MacAndrews & Forbes but did not terminate acquaintance with Perelman. Rifkind, a former judge of the United States District Court for the Southern District of New York and after 1950 a leading member of Paul, Weiss, was known as a great courtroom advocate. At eighty-one, he still had principal responsibility for certain clients, among them Lazard Frères and Revlon. Joseph Flom at Skadden, Arps had provided advice to Bergerac on another occasion. With these and other intermediaries, Bergerac felt Perelman could be dissuaded from going after the company in a hostile move. He was wrong.

On August 19 Revlon's board met to consider the situation. Of the fourteen Revlon directors, six, including Bergerac, held senior management positions in the company: Sander P. Alexander, senior vice president, finance, and chief financial officer, brought in by Bergerac from Champion International; Paul P. Woolard, senior executive vice president, Revlon's "marketing whiz"; and three other senior vice presidents and directors, including Irving J. Bottner, former president of Revlon's ultimate beauty salon division, the House of Revlon. The outside directors included Lewis L. Glucksman, former co-CEO of Lehman Brothers with Peter G. Peterson; Aileen Mehle, the gossip columnist from the *New York Daily News* known as "Suzy"; and Rifkind. At the meeting, Felix Rohatyn and William Loomis of Lazard Frères, Revlon's longtime investment banker, presented that firm's analysis.

According to the minutes of the board, Lazard Frères "approached Revlon both as a whole and also as the sum of its component parts." In each case, Revlon was analyzed from all financial perspectives — income statement, balance sheet, financial ratios, comparable transactions, and market prices. The analysis reaffirmed Bergerac's view that $45 per share was a grossly inadequate price for the company. Loomis also explained that Pantry Pride planned to acquire Revlon through junk bond financing, whereby Revlon's assets would secure the bonds and subsequently be sold to pay them off. It had been learned that Pantry Pride had retained Morgan Stanley to solicit purchasers for Revlon's various businesses. With proper timing, such a transaction could yield a return to Pantry Pride of $60 to $70 per share. On the other hand, a sale of the company as a whole would command a price in the mid-$50 range.

Perelman's intentions "were clear to every member of the Board," Rifkind later stated in an affidavit. "He wanted to buy Revlon at a wholesale price, sell the parts that he did not want at retail prices, and end up with the Beauty Products Division for a bargain price."

Lipton recommended defensive measures. First, the company should go into the open market to buy 5 million of its nearly 30 million outstanding shares of common stock, a program "designed to satisfy shareholder expectations of a market for their shares and to remove arbitrage pressure on the stock." Second, Revlon should adopt a note purchase rights plan, a variation on the poison pill defense.

Each Revlon shareholder would receive one note purchase right for each share of common stock, entitling the holder to exchange the share for a $65 Revlon note at 12 percent interest. The $65 figure approximated a rough cut at the price at which the board could liquidate the company or sell it whole to a third party. The note purchase rights would become effective if a bidder acquired a 20 percent stake, unless the bidder acquired all of the company's stock for cash at $65 or more per share. Thus the plan allowed shareholders other than a hostile bidder (such as Pantry Pride) to exchange their shares, or to "put" them back to the target for bonds worth about 40

percent more than the current stock price. An estimate reported in the *New York Times* said the plan could increase
the cost of purchasing the company by $750 million.

The board's minutes summarize Lipton's explanation: "The
Rights were designed not to interfere with a white knight
transaction prior to a 20% acquisition and to encourage potential bidders to negotiate with the Board. . . . The 20% . . .
ownership level approached the point where an acquiror might
be able to obtain *de facto* control of Revlon. . . . It would be
unlikely that someone could surprise the Company by becoming the . . . owner of 20% of the shares because of various
filing requirements under the securities and antitrust laws."
Another provision of the plan allowed Revlon's board to redeem the rights for 10 cents each anytime before a 20 percent
acquisition. Thus, when the danger of a takeover had passed,
the board could retire the rights cheaply. In effect, the rights
would compel a potential raider to negotiate with Revlon's board
rather than acquiring a significant stake in Revlon directly
from shareholders and then using that leverage to force a
merger. No shareholder would tender for less than $65 if he
would thus forfeit the opportunity to get a Revlon $65 note,
and so no tender offer less than $65 a share would be made.

Rifkind, reflecting on the meeting, said: "I had never before
voted for a poison pill device or advocated its use. Frankly, I
find the concept personally distasteful. But I argued in favor
of the proposal . . . because the alternative was even worse.
I did not wish to see Revlon's stockholders suffer, while Mr.
Perelman made a handsome profit by dismantling the company. In my view, Revlon's assets belonged to its shareholders, not to a liquidator."

The rights plan was a clever variation on the device used
by Unocal to force T. Boone Pickens to abandon his takeover
attempt. The Unocal strategy was a benefit package available
to all shareholders except the raider. Since that had been upheld, an antitakeover inducement that excluded the hostile
shareholder was fairly safe legally — at least for Delaware corporations. The Revlon rights plan allowed some but not others

of its shareholders to sell their shares back to the company at a premium. It was dubbed the "lollipop" because it "tastes good" to all shareholders except the hostile bidder. Unlike varieties of the poison pill that took effect only if the merger eventually occurred, the lollipop gave target shareholders monetary benefit as soon as the raider acquired 20 percent of the shares.

Wall Street debated whether the lollipop actually was harmful to shareholders' health. By giving the stockholder the right to exchange his shares for more valuable securities, the lollipop would drive away potential low bids. But once the threat passed, the company could drop the plan to buy back its stock, and that would result in a sharp fall in the stock's price, which would hurt the shareholders.

Felix Rohatyn noted an even more far-reaching consequence. While the rights could prevent tender offers at less than $65 per share, if a tender offer was made at that price or a higher one, the raider would have to recoup somehow. The only practical way to recoup would be to sell Revlon's assets. Hence, putting the rights in place would probably lead to liquidation of the company at a price somewhere near the $65 figure. And because the company could not support a price of $65 per share from its own cash flow, if Revlon itself had to pay that price, it too would be forced to sell assets.

The Revlon board nevertheless unanimously adopted the rights plan and the stock repurchase plan. As reported in the *Wall Street Journal,* "Revlon's Mr. Bergerac confirmed that the company recently has been approached by other companies. . . . 'The message that we have given to them is the company is not for sale. I am not soliciting offers. I don't want offers and we're not entertaining offers.' "

Perelman called Revlon's poison pill "a blatant attempt to deny its shareholders their right to decide for themselves whether or not to take advantage of Pantry Pride's cash tender offer." On August 22 Pantry Pride filed suit in Delaware state court, asking that the Revlon poison pill measures be declared invalid. A hearing was scheduled for September 10. Perelman

followed immediately with a cash tender offer at $47.50 per
common share for any and all shares of Revlon's 38.3 million
common shares outstanding, and $26.67 per preferred share
for its 100,000 preferred shares outstanding. The offer was
subject to two conditions. First, Pantry Pride must be able to
raise the $650 million necessary to buy the shares. Second,
the rights plan had to be withdrawn by Revlon or judicially
voided.

At $47.50 per share, Perelman was offering $1.8 billion for
Revlon. The *Wall Street Journal* speculated that Perelman expected a "quick killing." Pantry Pride issued a statement that
it could recoup its purchase price by selling off Revlon's
health care operations. The vision care division, which had a
strong position in the contact lens market, could bring as much
as $400 million. The Norcliff Thayer health products division,
which included Tums and medications for acne, could sell for
approximately $180 million. The medical diagnostic division
could bring $421 million. Revlon's weakest health care oper-
ation, prescription drugs, would probably sell for $600 million.
Its National Health Laboratories, one of the country's largest
chains of clinical labs, was highly profitable and could bring
a good price. If Pantry Pride sold all these units, it would still
be left with Revlon's cosmetics and toiletries operations, believed by some analysts to be worth at least $700 million.

Pantry Pride's intended public offering of securities was not
devoid of risk, and Pantry Pride acknowledged that it could
not meet debt service and dividend obligations for very long.
Perelman would have to take over another company that could
provide the required earnings. Perelman, it was said, "carves
it as close as he can."

On August 26 Revlon's directors met again. Based primarily
on the Lazard Frères presentation of a week earlier and on
this follow-up, they agreed to advise Revlon's stockholders
to reject Perelman's $47.50 per share offer as being too
low. Further defensive measures were also set in motion.
"If the Board were to do nothing," Lipton told the directors,

"in all likelihood Pantry Pride would acquire the shares at $47.50, particularly in light of the large arbitrage holdings of the stock."

On August 29, Revlon offered to repurchase up to 10 million of its common shares — 26 percent of those outstanding. Payment for each Revlon share was to be in a new note with a face value of $47.50, bearing 11.75 percent interest, and one tenth of a share of preferred stock with a value of $10, for a total value of $57.50. The company could pay off the shareholders over a period of time from cash flow.

The notes had provisions limiting Revlon's ability to incur additional debt, to sell assets, or to pay dividends except with the approval of Revlon's outside board members. "To vest important decision-making responsibility in persons other than Revlon management," said Rifkind, there was a provision that these covenants could be waived only by the "independent" directors, defined in the indenture as those directors holding office before a change in control. Since the notes would increase Revlon's debt by $475 million and sharply reduce shareholder equity, shares not tendered in the exchange would drop in value.

Lazard Frères, which designed these securities, maintained that the notes would trade in the marketplace at their face value of $47.50. In its letter to stockholders, Revlon stated that the exchange offer provided them "the opportunity to receive a substantial premium over recent market prices for a significant portion of their shares, while maintaining a continuing equity interest in the company."

Revlon's exchange offer was oversubscribed. The company accepted 10 million shares on a pro rata basis and in exchange issued $475 million in 11.75 percent notes and 1 million shares of the preferred stock. The tendering stockholders thereby became noteholders and preferred stockholders as well. Pantry Pride terminated its $47.50 per share tender offer but immediately made a reduced bid that took into account Revlon's offer. Pantry Pride's new offer was $42 per share for the stock apart from the notes, conditioned upon receiving at least 90 percent of the outstanding shares and the accompanying rights.

One way a raider can deal with poison pills is to gather enough of them that the dosage will not be fatal. To do this the raider can require the shareholder to tender not only the shares but also the warrant dividend, the pill. If the raider gets 90 percent of the shares, for example, he also gets 90 percent of the warrant dividends, leaving only 10 percent of the warrant dividends outstanding. The cost of dealing with this 10 percent may be measurable and controllable. Perelman's offer had this objective. While on its face lower than his earlier $47.50 proposal, Perelman's offer was essentially equal in value, given the effect of Revlon's prior exchange offer. William Loomis noted that "in its new offer, Pantry Pride had simply adjusted its original $47.50 price to take account of Revlon's purchase of 10 million shares and to reflect the premium that would likely be required to acquire the preferred stock issued in the Company Offer."

On September 24 Revlon's directors rejected the new Pantry Pride offer and authorized management to negotiate with other parties interested in acquiring the company. Undeterred, Perelman in a letter to Bergerac raised his offer to $50 cash per share, or $1.42 billion, if the antitakeover measures were dropped. "Dear Michel: . . . we remain convinced that a mutually agreed upon transaction is in the best interests of the stockholders of Revlon and Pantry Pride. To accomplish that result, we are prepared to enter into a merger agreement whereby all Revlon shareholders would receive $50 in cash for each of their common shares. Our proposal requires that Revlon's board redeem the 'poison pill' rights, [and] waive the covenants relating to sales of assets, incurrence of debt and restricted payments contained in the notes issued in Revlon's exchange offer. . . . We await your prompt response. Sincerely, Ronald."

On October 1, in another letter to Bergerac, Perelman increased the offer to $53 per share, conditioned on Revlon's approving the proposal at the board meeting that very night. "I can only describe the report to the Board [that evening] as bittersweet," said Rifkind. "We had begun with a Pantry Pride proposal in the low $40's, and now we could see the real possibility of a transaction in which the shareholders would be paid more than $53. But, at the same time, there was a sorrow in the realization that Revlon — as we had come to know it — might very well cease to exist." The board asked for an extension so that Pantry Pride's proposal could be considered along with other proposals in two days' time. Perelman granted the extension.

In the meantime, Lazard Frères was attempting to put together alternatives that might enable Revlon's shareholders to realize a higher price. Typically a company faces the twenty-day deadline for lining up a white knight. Also, the board has to worry about the bidder dropping the bid and doing a "street sweep"; that is, acquiring control of the target — by buying stock, primarily from arbitrageurs — in the marketplace. Revlon's situation was difficult. The company was in so many different lines of business that it could not easily find a single buyer who would operate it as a unit. Other buyers might not want the economic risk of selling the lines of business they did not want. A sale to a leveraged buyout group, on the other hand, might be feasible because such a group's business is buying and selling businesses. Late in the game, toward the end of September, Revlon secretly found its white knight.

o   o   o

Revlon had been meeting with two leveraged buyout firms, Forstmann Little, invited by Lazard Frères, and Adler & Shaykin. Leonard Shaykin of Adler & Shaykin proposed buying Revlon's cosmetic business at a price in the range of $850 to $900 million. With a number that high on the table, the possibility became real that the whole company could be sold in an LBO. Lazard could see $900 million coming from Adler & Shaykin without having to borrow on Revlon's other assets. The rest of the deal could be made with Forstmann Little. Accordingly, a package was proposed in which Forstmann

Little's deal was conditioned on the Adler & Shaykin deal, but the Adler & Shaykin deal was not conditioned on that with Forstmann Little. On this basis, an LBO of the rest of the company was possible at a price that could beat Perelman's.

On October 3 Revlon's directors considered Perelman's $53 bid. They also considered the proposal to sell the beauty products division to Adler & Shaykin, along with the Revlon name and trademark, and the rest of the company to a group headed by Forstmann Little.

Under Forstmann Little's LBO proposal, each Revlon stockholder would receive $56 cash per share. Financing would consist of the proceeds of selling the cosmetics business, bank loans, and $445 million in cash, for a total of $1.2 billion. The $445 million cash was to come in loans from pension funds of "conservative, well established organizations" including General Electric, Boeing, Standard Oil of Indiana, AT&T, General Telephone, and Texas Industries. The remainder of the financing was covered by bank commitment letters.

Also to help finance the deal, Forstmann Little reached an understanding to sell Revlon's Norcliff Thayer and Rehies divisions to American Home Products for $335 million immediately after the proposed merger. Most of Revlon's profitable health care businesses would be retained in a new company in which Bergerac and other Revlon management were to have an equity stake. This stake would be paid for by exercise of management's golden parachutes, already in place, which provided for substantial bonuses for managers and certain inside directors upon a change in control. Bergerac, for example, was to collect more than $20 million.

To facilitate the transaction, it was agreed that Revlon would redeem the warrant rights. In addition, Forstmann Little would assume the $475 million Revlon debt incurred by issuance of the notes. The note provisions that limited Revlon's ability to take on additional debt, sell assets, or pay dividends would be waived. However, counsel advised the board that if the pill was redeemed and the note restrictions were waived for Forstmann Little, the same would have to be done for anybody offering the same dollar amount or more. The restrictions on the notes, therefore, were unconditionally waived.

In response to a director's question regarding the effect of the waiver on the 11.75 percent notes, Martin Lipton commented that the notes "might not be as secure as they would be now and that there might be some complaint from bondholders." Added one director, "They should consider this as a package transaction, that the shareholders who had received the 11.75% Notes in the exchange offer were now receiving the benefit of the increased price for their shares. With respect to the buyers who had purchased the debt on the open market . . . [they] had taken the debt with full awareness of the possibility of the waiver of the covenants in the debt, and with the possibility that such steps might be taken in the context of the current circumstances surrounding the Company."

Felix Rohatyn, an independent director on numerous other boards, summarized the options before the board. The minutes note: "There was the $56 a share bid from Forstmann Little and the sale of the cosmetics business to Adler & Shaykin at $905 million. The only other bids that were on the table at that time . . . [were] the $42 a share Pantry Pride tender offer and its offer for a merger at . . . $53 a share. He stated that Forstmann Little's proposal was the only bid higher than Pantry Pride's to date. . . . that while a liquidation could possibly bring a higher price, a liquidation was not practical in view of Pantry Pride's possible purchases of shares [under its tender offer] the next day and . . . other risks of timing and consummation of a liquidation. He reminded the Board that he had originally indicated that the price range of a liquidation was $60 to $70 a share, and that the midpoint . . . was $65 a share. He noted that a 15% discount (which results in $56 a share) to eliminate the time factors and risks inherent in liquidation was reasonable. Thus, he had no qualms at all about recommending the $56 a share price being offered . . . without any financing conditions as an alternative to liquidation with all its problems and risks. . . ."

Forstmann Little's proposal was accepted by a unanimous

vote of the outside directors. Revlon's management directors absented themselves during much of the discussion and for this initial vote. When they returned to the meeting, a second vote was taken, and the result again was unanimous approval. A merger agreement between Revlon and Forstmann Little was promptly signed. A separate agreement covered the sale of Revlon's cosmetics and fragrance divisions to Adler & Shaykin for $905 million.

Perelman responded four days later by raising Pantry Pride's $53 offer to $56.25, 25 cents higher than the Forstmann Little bid. Perelman's new offer was conditioned upon the rights being nullified, the note provisions being waived, and three Pantry Pride directors being elected to the Revlon board. On October 9, Perelman informed Bergerac that Pantry Pride was prepared to top any Forstmann offer.

In the meantime, Forstmann Little, but not Pantry Pride, had been made privy to certain confidential Revlon financial projections. Ted Forstmann had also been afforded the opportunity to confer with Revlon's internal financial people about the company's accounting methods and controls. Such data could be useful, even if not indispensable, because internal financial details can more accurately reveal the value of a conglomerate's various components, and cash flow projections are the key to supporting a heavy debt burden.

Armed with this data, Forstmann Little was able to raise its bid to $57.25, subject to several conditions. Its principal demand was for an option to purchase Revlon's "crown jewel" vision care and National Health Laboratories divisions for $525 million. Subsequent testimony indicated that the price was $100 million to $175 million below the value given these divisions by Lazard Frères. This option, known as a lockup, gave Forstmann an advantageous position vis-à-vis a competitive bidder. Forstmann's lockup was to become a critical factor in the case.

o   o   o

In the more genteel Wall Street environment prevailing before hostile takeovers became respectable, it was safe to announce an acquisition months before final closing. A deal was a deal. By 1980, that was no longer possible. Any such announcement signaled to the marketplace that the target was for sale and often would provoke competing offers. By 1981, it was conventional wisdom in the "M & A" (mergers and acquisitions) business that no deal was safe from a competing offer. Faced with the threat of such competition, acquirers wanted to close fast, even in friendly deals, and, if possible, to arrange a lockup with the target.

"Lockup" perhaps overstates the effectiveness of the typical device: the term "leg up" is more accurate. A lockup does not guarantee that a deal will go through, nor does it prevent another bidder from stepping in. It simply increases the bidder's likelihood of success. In the early eighties several varieties had evolved, each structured more imaginatively than the one before.

The classic lockup was a stock purchase agreement whereby the bidder bought a significant block of the target's stock from one or several shareholders before news of the deal was made public. The bidder's ownership of these shares gave it power to prevent any other bidder from gaining control of the target. This strategy depended on there being a relatively small group of shareholders who owned a significant portion of the target's stock and who would support the proposed deal. Ideally, the bidder would purchase a majority of a target's outstanding shares this way, but even a 10 or 15 percent block could give the acquirer a leg up. The bidder's goal was to obtain an agreement from these shareholders that would hold even if there was a competing bid. If the stock of the rest of the shareholders was then bought at the same price, the bidder would gain by getting the company at its projected sum. Alternatively, if a competing bidder offered a higher price, the bidder could sell its stock to the competing bidder and realize a profit. If the bidder had determined the lockup price correctly, it had a "no lose" situation; nor were such arrangements often challenged in the courts.

If no block of stock was available, a bidder could seek an

arrangement with the target corporation itself. For example, the target's board could direct the company to sell stock to a friendly bidder or grant him an option to acquire shares. A "blank" class of preferred stock, with terms to suit the lockup, could be used instead of common stock. Or the target's board could grant an option on a strategically valuable company asset. The rationale for a crown jewel agreement was simple: A hostile bidder might become uninterested in a target whose key businesses had been sold away. Revlon gave Forstmann Little an asset lockup.

Revlon also was required to accept a "no shop" provision, prohibiting it from looking around for a better offer. In addition, a $25 million cancellation fee was to be placed in escrow and released to Forstmann Little if the new agreement fell through or if another entity acquired more than 19.9 percent of Revlon's stock. And the rights were to be redeemed and the restrictive note provisions removed.

In return, in addition to buying Revlon's stock at a somewhat higher price, Forstmann agreed to support the par value of Revlon's 11.75 percent notes. When the restrictions in the Revlon notes were waived in accordance with the merger agreement with Forstmann Little, there had been a resulting drop in the market price of the notes, reflecting the fact that the company would have a higher debt-to-equity ratio under the Forstmann Little deal. Rifkind was "deluged with telephone calls from irate [note] holders who had exchanged shares for 11.75% Notes which they believed would be worth par, and now saw a 13% erosion in the value of their Notes." Revlon's directors became increasingly concerned with restoring the notes' value. Forstmann promised to exchange the outstanding notes with new ones at a higher interest rate but demanded immediate acceptance of its offer.

Meanwhile, "rampant conflict of interest charges" against Bergerac appeared in the press. He responded by withdrawing as an investor in the leveraged buyout.

On October 12, Revlon's board convened to consider the situation as it had developed since the board's last meeting, on October 3. Perelman had increased Pantry Pride's offer by 25 cents over the Forstmann Little offer. However, Forstmann Little, figuring that Pantry Pride could top any further offer with a "nickel and dime" increase of its own, was willing to make a meaningful increase in its offer only if it received a lockup option.

Forstmann's proposal was unanimously approved by the Revlon board. Based on valuations given by Felix Rohatyn and William Loomis, the directors affirmed that Forstmann's proposal at $57.25 was more favorable to Revlon's shareholders than Pantry Pride's proposal at $56.25. According to the minutes of the board, "Forstmann Little stated that it would increase the price per share to $57.25 per share, but that it would require a lock-up at $525 million in the Vision Care and National Health Laboratories divisions." In addition to the price differential, Ted Forstmann's deal would protect the noteholders, a concern also reflected in the minutes. He "stated further that [Forstmann Little] . . . understood the concerns of the Company regarding the 11.75% Notes and that these concerns would be met by a proposed exchange offer." The minutes record that Forstmann concluded by saying "that he hoped the Board would not think him rude or pushy but that his offer was open only for this evening." Bergerac expressed concern that the unsettled situation was impairing Revlon's business operations and taking its toll on employee morale. The Forstmann proposal was unanimously approved.

Though the financing for the Forstmann Little deal was said to be firmly in place, there was a drawback. Forstmann's proposal had to be discounted for the time value of money. As a merger, it required shareholder approval. Approval was expected to take sixty days, a time lag that would make any immediate tender offer at the same price worth more to shareholders, and Pantry Pride's offer was immediate. Pantry Pride let it be known that Drexel Burnham, its investment banker, was confident of raising the balance of $350 million financing by October 18. But Pantry Pride acknowledged that its financing was not firmly committed.

Perelman was active on another front as well. On October 14, Pantry Pride filed an amended complaint in the Delaware court challenging the lockup in favor of Forstmann Little, the $25 million breakup fee to be paid if the merger failed, and the proposed retirement of the rights and waiver of the note provisions. It charged that the board's refusal to redeem the rights and the Forstmann lockup option deprived shareholders of a tender offer at a higher price than management's LBO. Pantry Pride sought a temporary restraining order to prevent transfer of assets to Forstmann. During the hearing on this request, the court was informed that some Revlon assets had already been placed in escrow; further transfers were prohibited.

The lower court struck down the lockup option, the no-shop provision, and the $25 million cancellation fee. Revlon's directors, the court found, had breached their fiduciary duty by effectively ending an active auction for the company. It also found a breach of duty in making concessions to Forstmann to protect the noteholders rather than maximizing the price that Revlon's stockholders were to receive for their stock.

In the interim, on October 18, Perelman had increased Pantry Pride's offer to $58 per share, again conditioned upon nullification of the rights plan and waiver of the note provisions. With this latest Pantry Pride offer pending and the Forstmann deal in abeyance as a result of the trial court's injunction, the Delaware Supreme Court on October 25, 1985, granted an expedited appeal.

o   o   o

Early on November 1, Delaware's Supreme Court affirmed. In the written opinion subsequently issued, the court took note of the "omnipresent specter that when implementing anti-takeover measures a board may be acting primarily in its own interests instead of those of the corporation and its shareholders." This possibility placed upon Revlon's directors the burden of proving that they had reasonable grounds, based on good faith and reasonable investigation, for believing that the Pantry Pride proposal threatened the corporation. Revlon's directors had failed to show that their actions were "reasonable in relation to the threat posed," the standard earlier adopted in the *Unocal* v. *Mesa Petroleum* case.

The rights plan as such was held proper. It was adopted in the face of an impending hostile takeover bid at $45 per share, a price that the board, on the basis of expert opinion, had reasonably concluded was grossly inadequate. In going that far the board had acted properly, the court concluded, for the rights plan left the door open to other proposals and was a factor in causing Pantry Pride eventually to raise its bid from $42 to $58. The court also upheld the second basic defensive measure, Revlon's August 29 notes exchange offer for 10 million of its shares. Since Revlon's directors reasonably concluded that Pantry Pride's $47.50 offer was "grossly inadequate," they acted properly in blocking it. In the court's opinion, however, the turning point came with the escalation of bidding.

When Pantry Pride increased its offer to $50 per share and then to $53, it became clear that the breakup of Revlon was inevitable. Rohatyn had warned early on that a high price per share would force a breakup of the company. Revlon's directors themselves had recognized that the company was for sale by authorizing management to negotiate a merger or buyout with a third party. Accordingly, in the view of the Delaware Supreme Court, the duty of the board thereupon changed from preserving Revlon as a corporate entity to maximizing the company's sale value for the stockholders' benefit. Defensive measures designed to prevent a bustup were misguided where the directors' role changed "from defenders of the corporate bastion to auctioneers charged with getting the best price for the stockholders at sale of the company."

When the board had become an auctioneer, the lockup with Forstmann Little, although it might have shored up the sagging market value of the notes, was inconsistent with the board's responsibilities to Revlon's shareholders. The notes' covenants specifically allowed for a waiver to permit the sale of Revlon at a fair price. Hence, the notes had been accepted with the risk of a drop in price resulting from a waiver. The board's sole objective should have been to obtain the highest price for the stockholders. By granting Forstmann Little the lockup, the Revlon board had ended the auction in return for insignificant improvement of the bid. According to the court, the directors were also improperly motivated by concern for their own possible personal liability to noteholders.

The lockup having been nullified by the court, Revlon accepted Pantry Pride's offer of $58 per share, or a total of about $1.8 billion. Since Revlon's directors were elected to staggered terms, without the company's cooperation Perelman would have needed up to two years to win control of Revlon's board. Cooperation was provided. Over the weekend of November 2–3, lawyers for the two companies negotiated an "orderly transfer" of control. Perelman agreed not to challenge the golden parachutes of key executives — even those who were to stay with the company — and gave his okay to the same exchange of notes as had Forstmann Little. He also agreed that shareholders who had not tendered would be paid at the same price. Last-minute discussions settled how Bergerac could retrieve the hunting scene mural in his inner office.

Bergerac opened his golden parachute totaling approximately $35 million, including a $7 million cash payment and $28 million in stock and stock options. Perelman took control of the Revlon board. Simon Rifkind, who had resigned from Revlon's board on account of conflict of interest during the struggle, was invited back. The publicly traded Pantry Pride, about a third of which was owned by Perelman's private holding company, MacAndrews & Forbes, acquired 100 percent of Revlon's shares. Pantry Pride changed its name to the Revlon Group, Inc.

By the end of 1986 Perelman had sold most of Revlon's divisions for a total of $1.4 billion, against the $1.8 billion price. Leonard Shaykin of Adler & Shaykin had expected to buy the Revlon beauty operations for $905 million. "I have no reason to believe the contract would not be honored," he said. "It's a breathtaking price." Perelman declared the agreement void, and Adler & Shaykin brought suit to enforce it, but just over a year later the case was settled for $23.7 million. Perelman put the beauty business back "on center stage."

Once Revlon's restructuring was completed, Perelman took the company private in a leveraged buyout. Sources contended that Perelman felt frustrated at having to satisfy the investment community. "Perelman was never one to exist well on . . . quarter-to-quarter analysis." In April 1987 Perelman agreed to pay $20.10 per share cash, a total of $850 million, to buy out the remaining approximately two thirds of Revlon stock that MacAndrews & Forbes did not already own. On that playing field that the court had taken such pains to level, Perelman's own holdings at $20.10 per share were worth $334 million. In eighteen months, Perelman had made more money by breaking up Revlon than Charles Revson had made in more than forty years of building it.

o   o   o

The rule of the *Revlon* case is that when directors are selling a company and an active bidding contest has developed, the auction must be conducted on a level playing field. Any arrangement with a bidder may be invalid if its purpose or effect chills competitive bidding.

But is there a difference between locking out competing bidders, which is not allowed, and drawing in a favorable bidder, which is allowed? Does a particular lockup maximize shareholder value or kill a higher bid? The answer can be found only in terms of the specific price for the lockup and the circumstances of the competition. Once the board has reached a decision to sell the company and another bidder has appeared, a director's primary duty becomes that of an auctioneer responsible for selling the company for the highest bid. However, obtaining that bid may require maneuvers whose legitimacy may later be questioned.

The Revlon situation involved a factor in addition to the lockup itself. The court found that in giving Forstmann Little preferred treatment, the directors were motivated in part by

fear of being held liable to the noteholders. Concern for that
interest was impermissible when the object no longer was to
maintain the corporate enterprise but to sell to the highest
bidder.

Should directors owe a fiduciary duty to bondholders? The
theory is that bondholders are sophisticated investors who hold
legally fixed obligations, which are specified in their contract.
Covenants protecting the revenues to pay the bonds can be
imposed on the borrowing company, and often are. Hence,
traditionally there has been no further duty to bondholders.
In contrast, an equity holder gets return only after fixed obligations are paid and if there is net revenue to pay dividends.
This difference means that, with regard to the bondholders,
the director is not managing other people's money, while with
regard to the stockholder, he is doing so. This is the basic
legal and financial difference between debt and equity.

In reality, the distinction is not so clean-cut. Rapid changes
in the economy can make obsolete the conditions under which
bonds were issued. And the increasing volatility of today's
capital markets can result in overnight transformation of the
financial condition of the company issuing the bonds. Moreover, Revlon bondholders were initially shareholders, and in
Revlon's exchange offer it was they who received subordinated debt. A few weeks later, when the restrictions on the
notes were waived, the market price of the notes severely declined. What kind of protection was that?

The question is equally relevant in the case of preferred
stock. A preferred stock investor in Revlon could not have
predicted that he was investing in an enterprise in which the
debt-to-equity ratio would be transformed into something like
9 to 1. And he was not protected against that transformation,
for usually there is nothing in the preferred stock provisions
to prohibit such a change. Should the preferred holders receive judicial protection in these circumstances, or — like a
noteholder — should they be dependent on the terms of their
preferred stock instrument?

The Delaware Supreme Court's opinion in *Revlon* also revalidated the use of poison pills. However, the court reiterated its admonition in *Moran* v. *Household International* that issuance of a pill initiates a bargaining process that displaces the market. As surrogate for the marketplace, the board must seek the highest price for all stockholders. And therefore, in the words of Revlon's counsel, the directors may not fix the race where they are "sponsoring one horse, particularly if management has a piece of that horse."

CHAPTER 6

o   o   o

On the Block:
Management Buyouts
and Open Bidding

INSIDE DIRECTORS and others on the management team
had a piece of the horse in both SCM's contest with Hanson Trust and Asher Edelman's contest with Fruehauf. That
directors place the stockholders' interests ahead of their own
is required in all cases, but especially when insiders have a
stake.

SCM Corporation in 1985 was a diversified conglomerate
best known for the Smith-Corona typewriter. On August 21,
its CEO, Paul Hamilton Elicker, received a hand-delivered letter from Lord Hanson, chairman of the board of Hanson Trust.
Lord Hanson had arrived in New York that week en route to
his Palm Springs home. The letter announced Hanson Trust's
intention to make a $60 all-cash tender offer for any and all
of SCM's common stock and said: "We would welcome the
opportunity to discuss how we can best effect our proposed
transaction for the benefit of your shareholders." Hanson also
issued a press release. SCM stock, which had been trading at
$46 just a few weeks earlier, went up 4⅛ to $64.13. Hanson
Trust had already purchased more than 87,000 shares, or about
1 percent of SCM common stock, at prices in the mid-$50
range. Analysts predicted that a higher bid would emerge from
either Hanson Trust or a new source.

Lord Hanson, né Mr. James Edward Hanson, was a York-
shireman and an avid huntsman. In the British press he was
known as "a master at the art of acquiring companies and
disposing of unwanted assets at a premium price." Knighted

in 1976, ennobled in 1983, James Hanson had made his maiden speech in the House of Lords in December 1983. He let others manage while he concentrated on strategy, always guided by caution. "I've always thought about the downside of risk on a take-over rather than the upside potential," he said. "We don't gamble."

Hanson Trust was formed in 1969 and quickly acquired what the *Financial Times* called a "formidable reputation in the City of London for turning problem companies round." Hanson Trust's business strategy had two components. The first was managing assets of industrial companies with the objective of reducing costs and generating cash. The second was trading in companies. These components were combined in the "Hanson legend," which was to borrow to buy a company, sell off part of its assets to pay the debt, and then push up earnings by tight management. Hanson's targets included mature low-technology businesses that were unlikely to require new capital, cyclical businesses on the downside, and companies whose profitability was slipping because of poorly performing divisions. In the years 1980–85, the value of Hanson Trust's stock had multiplied nearly thirteenfold, to $3.7 billion.

Lord Hanson's long-standing business partner, Sir Gordon White, also hailed from Yorkshire. In the late 1950s, a decade after a road-haulage operation owned by James Hanson's father was nationalized, Hanson and Gordon White went into business importing U.S. greeting cards. When British tax rates began to have "punitive effects," White immigrated to Bermuda and became Hanson Trust's man overseas. After combing Europe for investments, White decided to concentrate his efforts in the United States. "Six months among the French convinced me that their way of doing business wasn't my way." White had many interests, including parachute jumping, skiing, helicopter flying, bobsledding, and deal making. His apparent "insouciance about critical business affairs," friends said of him, hid a "fierce determination to win." Sir Gordon's outward gentility was said to contrast with the inner determination of "a hardened New York dealmaker." In Sir Gordon's

Park Avenue office was a painting of Lord Nelson's victory at Trafalgar, a fair indication of his temperament.

In just a decade from the time Hanson commenced operations in the States through its subsidiary, Hanson Industries, Sir Gordon became one of the most successful British investors in this country. Hanson Industries began in 1973 by buying a fish-meal company for $30 million. In 1976, it acquired Detroit's Hygrade Food Products, maker of Ball Park frankfurters. Hanson's most recent acquisition before it began stalking SCM was U.S. Industries, a multiline company, for which Hanson paid $520 million. Hanson Industries sales exceeded $2 billion, moving the subsidiary past the long-established Lever Brothers as the leading United Kingdom investor in the United States. Further acquisitions were needed for higher profits to meet increasing expectations of British shareholders.

Sir Gordon's attitude toward risk was the same as Lord Hanson's: "I have never considered what we could make on a deal but what we could lose." He also understood well how to raise money from banks. "They should be looking at the balance sheet of what we were buying . . . we could not secure the loans ourselves, but . . . we could secure them on the assets of our target companies." Sir Gordon was comfortable in America because "they do not understand the words 'no can do' . . . [i]t doesn't matter how stupid an idea you have, there is always someone who will listen and in many cases supply the capital." He himself never visited any of the U.S. group's operating companies. Said Sir Gordon, "There are no royal visits."

SCM Corporation, with executive offices just down the street from Sir Gordon's Park Avenue outpost, was a diversified, multinational conglomerate chartered under New York law. The company had more than seventy plants around the world in businesses which included office machinery, chemicals, paints, paper products, and food processing. Labeled a Wall Street "glamour stock" during the 1960s, SCM was later called a "second rate conglomerate with some first rate parts." In

1980 SCM had been the target of Royal Little of Textron and Willard Rockwell, former chairman of Rockwell International. Through long legal battles, however, it had preserved its independence. Thereafter, SCM's typewriter operations continued to lose money. Earnings dropped from a peak of $56.5 million in 1981 to $24.5 million in 1983.

By 1985 SCM's fortunes were turning. Its specialty chemicals and coatings businesses accounted for more than half of its $2.2 billion in sales and four fifths of its operating profits. Within the chemicals group, the pigments division was one of the four leading world producers of titanium dioxide. Its foods division was the second-largest full-line spice processor and distributor in the United States; within that division was Durkee Famous Foods, which sold a wide variety of popular spices, extracts, gravy mixes, and other consumer products. Pigments and Durkee Famous Foods, called SCM's "crown jewels" by Hanson, together generated approximately 50 percent of SCM's net operating income. Hanson, "as a consequence of the culling which our people are always going through," caught SCM near the end of a heavy capital spending program but before the investment paid off.

Hanson's cash tender offer of $60 per share for any and all shares put a value on SCM of approximately $755 million. On August 22, a day after the offer was submitted, Elicker asked Goldman, Sachs, SCM's financial advisers, and Wachtell, Lipton, retained five years previously in a proxy contest, to "come in and consult with us." Elicker was advised that Lord Hanson's letter did not call for a reply. On August 22 Reuters reported Elicker's position: "We think we can provide shareholder value by . . . continuing an independent role . . . I think the shareholders deserve that. We have done pretty well for them."

Testifying later, Elicker said: "We judged by the facts of the case and not by what a letter might happen to say, and if the facts of the case were that we had a situation where a clearly inadequate offer was made, a low bid in a hostile tender offer under time pressure, everything about that says it is not a negotiating circumstance. . . . The Hanson Trust reputation was that they did do lowball offers and it was much more likely we would get more value for the stockholders if we went to a competing offer if we could find it."

Q: — Was there any discussion among your advisors as to the question of whether you should or should not pursue Hanson negotiations?

A: — We discussed that this letter had the characteristics I described, and that it was very unlikely that . . . they would top their own offer. Everything indicated the reverse. . . .

Q: — Did your advisor say anything . . . as to what impact it would have on other potential offerors if the word got out that you were trying to negotiate with Hanson? . . .

A: — Absolutely.

Q: — What was that decision?

A: — It was going to be difficult to find other people, and . . . we could not . . . give the implication we were using [Lord Hanson] . . . as a stalking horse to get the Hanson bid up. That would mean that the bid was not going to materialize.

Q: — From others?

A: — Yes.

SCM's advisers explained the necessity of SCM's finding an alternative quickly. Several were considered, among them a leveraged buyout in which SCM management would participate. Separate discussions were opened with Kohlberg, Kravis, Roberts & Company and Merrill Lynch Capital Markets. Having been one of SCM's investment bankers for several years, Merrill Lynch was already familiar with the company's financial condition. Elicker called each SCM director to discuss the situation. None suggested that SCM contact Hanson to see whether it would raise its bid.

On Sunday, August 25, SCM's twelve-member board met for the first time to discuss Hanson's offer and SCM's strategies. Aside from Elicker, then sixty-two, a graduate of Yale

College and the Harvard Business School who had joined SCM nearly thirty years before, the board included two other SCM managers: D. George Harris, president and chief operating officer, who would be part of the proposed LBO group; and senior vice president George E. Hall. Of the nine outside directors, none had a significant holding of SCM common stock, and all had considerable business experience and working knowledge of SCM and its operations.

Goldman, Sachs distributed a document analyzing the Hanson offer, concluding that $60 was an inadequate price for SCM and that Hanson had the money to finance its offer. The board formally retained Goldman, Sachs and Wachtell, Lipton to seek a white knight or a leveraged buyout. Because SCM was a highly diversified conglomerate, it would be difficult to find a company that would see an immediate fit with all of SCM's existing lines. Lipton therefore recommended that the board also consider a leveraged buyout by a group centered in SCM's management. The board delegated to management the responsibility of exploring both options with the advice of Willard Overlock, Jr., and Lipton. Meetings between Merrill Lynch and numerous representatives of SCM's management began immediately and continued over the next few days. Representatives of Kohlberg, Kravis also visited.

Hanson now made a further move through its financial adviser, Robert S. Pirie, president and CEO of Rothschild Inc. and a former Skadden, Arps takeover lawyer. Pirie asked Lipton to assure Elicker that Hanson Trust and White were "good people" and to arrange for Elicker to meet with White to work out SCM's acquisition by Hanson Trust. Lipton declined. His previous experiences with Hanson Trust and White led him to think they were not "good people," and he refused to act as intermediary.

Other attempts by Hanson to reopen discussions with SCM also failed. Elicker's views were no secret. Commenting on Wall Street "players" who "made money by trading bits of paper back and forth in the frenzy of takeover battles," Elicker told security analysts: "This contributes nothing to America's growth or to our economic strength as a nation . . . [but] deterring the energetic pursuit of such gains is probably like trying to make water run uphill."

Meanwhile, Goldman, Sachs contacted more than forty companies to seek out a white knight. As anticipated, none was willing. Of the three LBO firms contacted by August 30, only Merrill Lynch Capital Markets had expressed interest.

Agreement on an LBO was quickly reached with Merrill Lynch, subject to SCM board approval. Through a corporate shell called ML SCM Acquisition, Inc., Merrill Lynch would make a $70 tender offer for up to 10.5 million SCM shares, approximately 85 percent of the company's outstanding shares. In a second step, the remaining shareholders would exchange their shares for subordinated debentures — junk bonds — valued at $70 per share. Or the remaining shareholders could resort to their appraisal rights under New York law, which allow stockholders to be paid for their shares in a court-supervised appraisal rather than having to accept the price offered in the proposed exchange.

The LBO would be $59.50 per share in cash and $10.50 in newly issued debentures. At trial Kenneth Miller, a managing director of Merrill's Capital Market Group, was cross-examined about the LBO by Dennis J. Block of the New York law firm of Weil Gotshal & Manges, representing Hanson Trust.

Q: — . . . Are the assets of SCM being utilized in connection with the borrowing?

A: — Well, the funds that are being used to pay for the tender offer are coming largely from Merrill Lynch and Prudential.

Q: — And?

A: — And then subsequently . . . it would be refinanced with a bank debt. . . .

Q: — Basically . . . the borrowing power that the assets of SCM can generate would be used to pay for part of the transaction?

A: — In part, yes.

Q: — That's not the case, as you know, in either of the Hanson offers, right?

A: — I don't know that at all. I would assume that in fact they are relying on the same economic values as we are to finance their offer.

SCM management was given the right to purchase up to 15 percent of the new ML SCM Acquisition Inc. Miller was asked who was in that group, and he replied: "I think that's yet to be defined . . . how broadly it will be cast and so forth. That's all being negotiated. But they will get an equity ownership interest in the new company."

Q: — And this is the management group that doesn't want Hanson Trust, it wants Merrill Lynch. . . .

A: — I wouldn't have put it that way. I would say they don't want control of the company stolen in the open market.

Merrill Lynch, which was financing management's buyout, would hold a large equity stake. It insisted on "protective measures" to assure receiving some benefit whatever the outcome. SCM's management granted Merrill Lynch a $1.5 million engagement fee (a "hello" fee) and a $9 million breakup fee (a "good-bye" fee), which meant, in Elicker's words, that "if they don't get the company they are making the bid for, they get another $9 million for leaving, going away." The hello fee was to be paid immediately. The good-bye fee was payable if any third party acquired one third or more of SCM's outstanding shares for $62 or more per share before March 1, 1986. The rationale was that such an acquisition could block the planned merger into the new Merrill Lynch entity, since under New York corporation law a merger requires the approval of two thirds of the outstanding shares entitled to vote. The fee was contingent on SCM's having received a bid higher than Merrill Lynch's.

As Elicker testified:

Q: — Merrill Lynch wanted the break-up fee triggered by the acquisition of one-third, so if somebody else obtained a blocking position and Merrill didn't get a two-thirds vote on the merger Merrill Lynch could walk away with a $1.5 million fee?

A: — They certainly didn't want to do all this work with no
    result.

On Friday, August 30, just before the Labor Day weekend,
the Merrill Lynch LBO proposal was presented to SCM's board
through a conference call. All nine of the outside directors
took part. Elicker, Hall, and Harris from SCM management
and the representatives from Goldman, Sachs and Wachtell,
Lipton participated from SCM's offices. The board was advised that Merrill Lynch was prepared to commit $450 million
of equity and subordinated debt financing with good prospects for additional financing from the Prudential Insurance
Company. The proposal was summarized in a two-page letter
agreement and described in detail to the nine outside directors. However, the letter agreement itself was not put in the
directors' hands until after the directors had authorized SCM
management to negotiate a definitive merger agreement. The
three management directors did not vote.

The merger agreement, negotiated over Labor Day weekend, was presented to a special meeting of the board on September 3. Overlock explained that it was the only counter to
Hanson's still-outstanding $60 bid. He delivered Goldman,
Sachs's opinion that Merrill Lynch's $70 bid was "fair" to SCM
shareholders and proposed that the debentures for the remaining stockholders be priced by consensus of Goldman,
Sachs and Merrill Lynch or, if they disagreed, by a third investment banker to ensure that their fair value was $70 per
share. The SCM board understood that some as yet unidenti-
fied SCM officers would participate in the LBO through an
equity position of up to 15 percent. The nine outside directors
unanimously approved the merger agreement. The three
management directors, Elicker, Hall, and Harris, though
present at the meeting, again did not vote.

At the closing later that day, Elicker was advised that Hanson had issued a press release raising its tender offer to $72
cash, conditioned on SCM's granting no lockup agreements
or options to any other bidder. The price was higher than

Merrill's offer and had no "back-end paper," i.e., junk bonds. SCM's management, Overlock, and the lawyers from Wachtell, Lipton caucused. At trial, Block questioned Elicker about these discussions.

Q: — You all determined that the thing to do was to go back to Merrill Lynch to see if they would raise their offer?

A: — That's right.

Q: — Nobody said a word: Gee, [Hanson] just increased their bid by 20 percent or $12 a share; maybe they will go even a little higher to wrap this thing up? Nobody said even that?

A: — No. There was no indication that that would be a thing that anyone would say.

In the face of Hanson's new offer, however, SCM and Merrill Lynch terminated their pending agreement and entered negotiations for a revised version. The events were reviewed at trial.

Q: — Who specifically went back to Merrill Lynch?

A: — The negotiation with Merrill Lynch was conducted by Goldman, Sachs and Wachtell.

Q: — You were present.

A: — I was not present. We supplied information, additional information, factual, as they needed it.

Q: — Merrill Lynch took the position if it were to bid $74 they wanted lockup options, right?

A: — That's correct. . . .

Q: — They told you they wanted the pigments segment of the chemical business, correct?

A: — Yes.

Q: — And they told you they wanted the consumer food business of your food division, correct?

A: — That's right.

Q: — You regard the pigments business as the most important part of the company, correct?

A: — . . . It's a very important part of the company. . . .

Q: — Merrill said to you: In order for us to go above $72 we need a lockup. Did it occur to you that maybe you should call Hanson at that point and ask them if they would go above $72 without a lockup?

A: — It didn't make sense. . . .

Q: — Merrill Lynch ultimately agreed to make a new proposal, correct?

A: — Eventually.

Q: — Merrill agreed to make a proposal of $74 per share, correct?

A: — That's right.

Q: — But that proposal didn't involve Merrill putting up one single penny in additional cash above their $70 offer, isn't that correct?

A: — I don't recall a penny. Essentially most of the increase was in debentures, that's correct. . . .

Q: — Merrill was now offering in essence $60 in cash and $14 in back-end paper instead of the $60 cash.

A: — That's [it] at least approximately.

In a letter dated September 10 to Elicker, White had again urged discussion of a "friendly" takeover. Elicker refused.

On the same day, the new SCM–Merrill Lynch proposal was presented at an SCM board meeting that began at nine o'clock at night and lasted till about midnight. Merrill proposed a $74 cash tender offer for at least two thirds and up to 80 percent of SCM's common stock. The cash tender would be followed by a second-step merger in which each of the remaining 20 percent of SCM's shares would be exchanged for debentures valued at $74. The proportionate cash component of this offer was $59.20 per share, 30 cents less than under the earlier offer, while the debt component was $4.30 more.

SCM also agreed to give Merrill Lynch the $9 million good-bye fee, an additional $6 million "hello again" fee for making the revised proposal, and, most important, a lockup option on SCM's crown jewels — Pigments and Durkee Famous Foods. Under the proposed lockup option, if a third party acquired more than one third of SCM's common stock, Merrill Lynch could purchase Pigments for $350 million and Durkee Famous Foods for $80 million.

On cross-examination at trial, Kenneth Miller was asked by Block:

Q: — Do you know what a lockup is, Ken?

A: — No, what is a lockup, Dennis.

Q: — What do you think it is?

A: — What do you think it is?

Q: — I think a lockup is a transaction in which one party is given an opportunity to purchase either for cash or an option to purchase in the future an asset of the company. Do you accept that?

A: — I don't accept that, no.

Q: — What would you describe it as?

A: — Well, I don't use the expression. What I think happened here was that Merrill Lynch, as a condition for raising its offer beyond a level that advisers to Hanson had characterized as generous, insisted on the right to buy two businesses for a fair price.

Q: — Without regard to the price, you would concede to me that you now had a right to take those businesses out of SCM if in fact certain contingencies took place?

A: — We do have such a right, yes.

Q: — Is it your experience as a man who has been practicing investment banking for at least ten years that that kind of operation affects the bidding, some people say it chills the bidding; do you think that that's true?

A: — I have seen it happen both ways.

Overlock advised that the $74 Merrill Lynch offer was the best available, that it was fair to SCM shareholders, and that the option prices for the crown jewels were "within the range of fair value," but he did not quote a range. According to the minutes of the meeting, Overlock told the board that the option price of $350 million for Pigments represented 25 percent over book value and that the option price of $80 million for Durkee represented 43.6 percent over book value. "In keeping with Goldman, Sachs' regular practice in valuations of this type," Overlock later affirmed, "information relating to [Durkee] Famous [Foods] and Pigments was prepared and distributed to various members of the Mergers and Acquisitions Department, whose views as to the range of values for each business were solicited and considered. Goldman, Sachs' internal procedures require that at least two partners in the Mergers and Acquisitions Department must agree on the fairness of the price before the firm may give its opinion, and in this case that procedure was followed."

However, Overlock told the board that he believed SCM could obtain a higher price for each business if an orderly sale was conducted. Overlock also told the board that "the current trading value" of Merrill Lynch's $74 offer would be above $72 per share. The point was later reviewed at trial, Block questioning Elicker:

Q: — Overlock told the board on the night of September 10 that the current trading value of the Merrill Lynch transaction would be above $72 per share, but he did not say it would be $74 per share, correct? . . . The reason for that is . . . that the first 80 percent or 90 percent of the stock . . . would take about a month to a month and a half to actually be purchased and that the back-end debentures, the 20 percent, would take as much as 3 months to be issued, correct?

A: — From an arbitrageur's point of view, that's correct.

Q: — How about from the point of the little shareholder . . . he is not going to get his piece of paper for 3 months, is that correct?

A: — That's correct, but he is going to get $74 when he does.

Q: — Mr. Elicker, he is going to get $74 for the first 80 percent of his pieces of paper he is going to tender to you, correct?

A: — That's correct.

Q: — And then three or four months later when this merger takes place, he is going to be handed another certificate, that 20 year no interest for 5 year piece of paper, and that is going to be three months later or so, correct?

A: — That's right. . . . He is going to get $74, some part of which he is going to get later.

Q: — . . . He won't have his money for three months, right?

A: — That's right.

Q: — As a business person you know not having money has a cost, right, when you borrow, you have to pay interest, right?

A: — Yes.

Q: — And you know there is a difference between current value of money and future value of money, correct?

A: — Yes. . . .

Q: — Has any member of the board of directors of SCM asked or commented about how this three-month delay reduced the value of the back end piece of paper? Did anyone raise that question?

A: — It was discussed as to how arbitrageurs would look at it, yes, as being a value in excess of $72, not the full $74, to them, not as I indicated, to the individual shareholder as such who was getting $74. . . . The arbitrageur looks at those differently from the shareholder.

During the board meeting, Lipton had advised that approving the lockup was within the board's "business judgment." When a director asked whether Merrill Lynch would proceed with its $74 proposal without the lockup option, Merrill Lynch's chief negotiator responded that it would not. The three management directors left the room; the outside directors unanimously approved the lockup agreement.

Next day Hanson withdrew its $72 offer. Hanson also proceeded to buy more SCM common stock, now at $73.50 per share, bringing its holdings to approximately 25 percent. On September 20, Hanson filed suit in the United States District

Court for the Southern District of New York, seeking an injunction against the Merrill Lynch transaction and alleging that SCM's directors had breached their fiduciary duties and had wasted SCM's assets in the agreement with Merrill Lynch.

Within two weeks Hanson purchased an additional 545,000 shares of SCM stock, increasing its holdings to 37.4 percent. This foreclosed the possibility that the SCM–Merrill Lynch management LBO could gain the necessary approval by holders of two thirds of its shares. On October 8, Hanson announced a $75 cash tender offer for all remaining shares of SCM, conditioned on withdrawal of the lockup and return of the $9 million breakup fee. Merrill Lynch countered by announcing that it would exercise the lockup option and withdraw the $9 million from escrow. Hanson then dropped the demand for return of the escrow fund, yielding to Merrill Lynch what Hanson apparently hoped would be a forever good-bye fee.

A serious new risk now loomed. The market price of SCM shares would be likely to fall precipitously if both Hanson's new cash tender offer and Merrill Lynch's offer were to fail. To provide a safety net, the SCM board on October 10 approved an exchange offer, to begin October 18, in which SCM shareholders could exchange each SCM share for $10 cash and $64 in a new series of SCM preferred stock. The offer was to be made for two thirds of the company's outstanding shares. If the Merrill offer was consummated, all the shares tendered would be treated as tendered into the Merrill Lynch offer.

In the pending lawsuit, Hanson moved for an injunction to prohibit Merrill Lynch from exercising the option to buy SCM's Pigments and Durkee businesses. To give the court time to deliberate, Merrill Lynch agreed to wait temporarily. Hanson thereupon commenced its previously announced $75 cash tender offer, still subject to the proviso that the merger agreement and lockup be nullified by the court or by SCM itself.

When SCM's board met three days later, it rejected the new Hanson offer on the grounds, among others, that it "includes

as conditions the abrogation of contractual arrangements that
the board entered into for the benefit of shareholders and which
. . . are valid and binding." The board ratified its own exchange offer for $10 cash and $64 in preferred stock and recommended that shareholders accept either that offer or the
offer by Merrill Lynch. Hanson thereupon asked the court to
enjoin implementation of this proposal. There things stood,
awaiting decision by the court.

o   o   o

In court, all parties professed concern for the interests of
SCM's shareholders. In a trial record spanning thirty volumes, Hanson argued that it wanted to give the SCM shareholders the highest price for their equity; Merrill Lynch argued that it obtained the lockup option to create additional
value for SCM shareholders; the senior members of SCM's
management, who were to participate in the leveraged buyout, said they too were concerned "with securing the greatest
value for SCM shareholders"; SCM's board and the financial
and legal advisers on all sides were of the same voice. Some
shareholders disagreed and brought a shareholders' derivative
suit, which was assigned to another judge of the same court.

On November 26, 1985, Judge Shirley Wohl Kram held
against Hanson. She concluded that Merrill Lynch would not
have proceeded without the option to buy SCM's two key
businesses, and that without Merrill Lynch's $74 offer, Han-
son would not have offered $75 per share. The directors,
therefore, approved the lockup options only "after concluding
that they could not secure the $74 LBO offer without the op-
tions." Moreover, the court found that the lockup option prices
were the product of "arm's-length negotiations" between
Goldman, Sachs and Merrill Lynch. Although there were
"several aspects of the independent directors' actions which
trouble the court," said Judge Kram, the board's decision was
within the scope of its business judgment. She denied Hanson's request that the court enjoin SCM and Merrill from exercising the lockup option.

Hanson immediately appealed to the United States Court of

Appeals for the Second Circuit. The appeal was expedited, being argued on December 18 and decided on January 6, 1986. The decision addressed a basic principle: that free market forces ordinarily should determine the bargaining outcome. On the one hand, said the Court of Appeals, lockup options are not per se illegal, since they sometimes benefit shareholders by inducing a good bid. On the other hand, said the court, lockup options that shut out competing bidders are harmful.

According to Circuit Judge Lawrence Pierce, whether to grant a lockup ordinarily involved a business judgment that a court would not second-guess. However, the business judgment rule could not prevent inquiry into directors' acts where their "methodologies and procedures" were "so restricted in scope, so shallow in execution, or otherwise so pro forma or halfhearted as to constitute a pretext or sham." While finding that the actions of SCM's directors did not fall to the level of "gross negligence," so that they were not personally liable in damages, the court nevertheless held that the LBO should be enjoined.

Its basis of decision was that the SCM board had breached its duty of care when, in fending off one acquirer, it agreed to sell the company's most prized assets to another at bargain prices. The court found that the SCM board's decision on September 10 to sell Pigments and Durkee Famous Foods was made in great haste, after a three-hour late-night meeting in which SCM's investment bankers had provided neither a written opinion on the value of the businesses nor a range of values for the board to consider. The SCM board never asked why the two crown jewel businesses, which generated half of SCM's income, were being sold for one third of the total purchase price. Rather than requesting documentation respecting the investment banker's opinion, the board merely accepted a conclusion that the option prices were "within the range of fair value." Nor had the directors suggested postponing a decision on the lockup option. The court noted that Hanson would not have actually acquired shares under its offer until September 17, a week beyond the September 10 board meeting. That would have left ample time to give more careful consideration to the price estimates for Pigments and Durkee.

The court was unpersuaded that SCM's "working board" was sufficiently familiar with the company to make swift decisions concerning such important issues. If the board had such familiarity, asked the court, why did it not find the lockup option prices troublesome? The option price properly may be "low enough to entice a reluctant potential bidder," but it must be no lower than "reasonable pessimism will allow." Nor had the board asked whether SCM would remain a going concern if these two businesses were sold.

Also relevant was the fact that the outside directors were dealing with a self-interested management in the defensive LBO. As Judge Pierce said, it would be "unreasonable to expect management, with financial expectancies in an LBO, fully to represent the shareholders." In a concurring opinion, Judge James Oakes observed that when management interests are in direct conflict with interests of target corporation shareholders, "the director's duty of care is heightened." Yet SCM's board gave management broad authority to work directly with Merrill Lynch to structure the LBO and then quickly approved management's proposals. Even after Wachtell, Lipton was formally retained by the board, there was sufficient confusion for a Prudential Insurance negotiator to note in a confidential diary: "Lipton rep[resentin]g m[ana]g[emen]t" (additions in brackets are the court's).

As the court saw it, the SCM–Merrill Lynch LBO could benefit shareholders only if it succeeded all the way through the merger stage and if the new entity was a financial success. If the buyout fell short of its ultimate goal, nontendering shareholders could bear all of the potential risk, being left only with appraisal rights. If the plan failed at the first stage because the required two thirds did not tender, half the company was still to be sold to Merrill Lynch for an inadequate price. Beyond this, the $16.5 million in hello and good-bye fees represented a dissipation of approximately $1.25 per share.

The Court of Appeals put the question raised in *Revlon*: "What motivated the directors to end the auction with so little objective improvement?" The court's conclusion was that the board must have wanted the LBO participants "in the picture at all costs."

The order of the District Court was reversed. Hanson proceeded with its offer of $75 per share and by January 7 had acquired about two thirds of SCM's shares. Following shareholder approval, the merger became effective on March 31, 1986, for a total price of approximately $922 million. Hanson Trust recouped $930 million by selling several businesses, among them Glidden Paint for $580 million to IC Industries. Hanson kept the typewriter business and other SCM businesses, including Pigments and Durkee Famous Foods. Effectively it paid nothing for them. Some "efficient market"!

o   o   o

The legal protection that shareholders need in a management buyout, and that by law they should have, clashed with the realities of a buyout transaction on yet another playing field. In February 1986, while Hanson was selling the SCM businesses, a group of investors organized by Asher Edelman, a forty-six-year-old arbitrageur turned corporate raider, began buying Fruehauf Corporation's stock on the open market. Edelman had told *Barron's* that as the field of risk arbitrage had become crowded, "I began to look for an alternative that would have the kind of risk/reward that I wanted." Takeovers were the answer: "If the analytical skills . . . were relatively the same . . . why not be the mover instead of betting that other people will be the movers. And that's when I went into the 13D business." He was referring to SEC Schedule 13D, the disclosure statement that must be filed by an investor when he has acquired 5 percent or more of a company's stock.

In 1983, Edelman acquired Canal-Randolph, a commercial real estate concern, and then spun off a stockyard subsidiary and sold several properties, making $30 million in profit on a $23 million investment. His next move was in the computer field. In a hard-fought proxy contest he won control of Management Assistance, which made and serviced small computers, reaping another $11 million in profit. On the other hand, he did poorly with Mohawk Data Sciences Corporation, which lost more than 70 percent of its value after he acquired it. An investment in Datapoint Corporation suffered a similar fate. No matter; Edelman saw Fruehauf as an excellent opportunity.

The Detroit-based Fruehauf, incorporated under the laws of Michigan, was a leading producer of truck trailers and cargo containers. It also owned a finance company, manufactured auto parts and container-handling equipment, and did ship construction and repair. Its 1985 sales of $2.5 billion yielded $70 million in net profits. In February 1986 Fruehauf's shares were trading in the mid-$20 range.

By March 1986 Edelman had acquired 9 percent of Fruehauf's 22 million shares for prices ranging from $26.75 to $38 per share. Three times he attempted unsuccessfully to meet with Fruehauf's board to negotiate a "friendly" acquisition. His demand for a stockholder list was rejected, as was a suggestion that he have representation on the company's board.

When this approach failed, Edelman proposed a cash merger in which Fruehauf shareholders would receive $41 per share, or a total of $812 million. Edelman began soliciting proxies on April 3 to elect a rival slate of directors at Fruehauf's annual shareholders' meeting, scheduled for May 1. Fruehauf, in a full-page advertisement, urged its shareholders to vote against Edelman's candidates, who were pledged to help put through his $41 per share offer.

In a letter to Fruehauf's board dated April 20, Edelman raised his offer to $42 per share. The proposal was rejected. On May 1, Fruehauf announced that its shareholders had overwhelmingly reelected management's nominees to the board. Edelman "was humiliated by a lopsided vote in favor of management," the press reported. But, he promised shareholders, "I shall return."

On June 11, 1986, Edelman announced a cash tender at $44 per share. Since Fruehauf shares were then trading at above $45, Wall Street presumed the bid would be raised. A special meeting of the Fruehauf board was held on the same day; Neal Combs, executive vice president and likely successor to Robert Rowan as CEO, led a discussion of various alternatives. Their preferred option was a leveraged buyout that would leave management in control while allowing Edelman to tender his shares at a comfortable profit. Rowan, Combs, and other members of Fruehauf's management opened negotiations with Merrill Lynch Capital Markets for a management buyout "in the area of $50 per share."

As the court ultimately found, Fruehauf's share value was well in excess of $50 per share, but "Rowan and Combs informed their advisers that they did not wish to participate in the buy-out at a price above first $48 and then $48.50." When the board met again on June 19, an LBO proposal from management and Merrill Lynch was submitted, without written analyses or evaluations or even a suggested price. The board nevertheless immediately supported the proposal, and a special committee of outside directors was appointed to evaluate it in relation to Edelman's offer. Kidder, Peabody and the law firm of Shearman & Sterling, with Dennis Friedman acting as field general, were to advise the committee.

Five days later, the management LBO was approved, although no attempt had been made to negotiate the terms directly with Merrill Lynch. Merrill Lynch had been willing to pay $50 per share, and Kidder, Peabody had evaluated the stock at a still higher price, but these facts were not disclosed to the board. Reliance had been placed on Kidder, Peabody and management to negotiate on behalf of the shareholders, inasmuch as the special committee members felt that, as they later testified, they "lacked the expertise to interfere with negotiation of the transaction."

At the same June 24 meeting, the board unanimously approved acceleration of all management stock options if a raider purchased 40 percent of the company's shares. The corporation's incentive compensation plan also was amended so that a raider's purchase would make all sums due under the plan immediately payable. The pension plan was amended so that its surplus, valued at between $70 million and $100 million, would be insulated from a raider but remain available for a management leveraged buyout.

The following day, the plan was announced. A corporation was to be formed to purchase approximately 77 percent of Fruehauf's stock for $48.50 per share cash. The purchase was to be funded by loans totaling $750 million from Merrill Lynch Capital Markets and Manufacturers Hanover, with another $100 million to be advanced by Fruehauf Corporation itself. Fruehauf would then be merged into the acquiring corporation. Fruehauf shareholders beyond the 77 percent would receive securities in the new corporation, valued by Kidder, Peabody at $48.50.

Total equity contribution to the new company would be only $25 million dollars — $10 million to $15 million from management, for which it would receive between 40 and 60 percent of the new company, and the rest from Merrill Lynch. Fruehauf also was to pay Merrill Lynch approximately $30 million in loan commitment fees, advisory fees, and a breakup fee that Merrill Lynch would keep if the transaction did not go through. The package included a no-shop clause restricting Fruehauf's ability to negotiate a better deal with another bidder.

According to *Business Week,* the deal would leverage Fruehauf to the hilt even though its debt already was 50 percent of equity. Although the company had a strong cash flow, its business was cyclical, 1985 sales were off, and earnings had dropped — trends that were likely to continue.

Before the management offer could be mailed to shareholders, the Edelman group offered a similarly structured merger for $49.50 per share, a dollar more, and proposed as an alternative to buy all outstanding shares for $49.50 per share cash. Both offers were subject to two conditions: obtaining financing and the Fruehauf board's endorsement of the proposal. The Edelman group was confident it could come up with the money. Edelman's offer was discussed in a conference-call meeting of the Fruehauf board's special committee and representatives of Kidder, Peabody and Shearman & Sterling. Without referring the matter to the full board, the special committee concluded that Edelman's proposal should be rejected unless it was fully funded — in the words of one committee member, unless Edelman "put his money on the table."

At this point, a member of Edelman's group brought a stockholders' derivative suit in the U.S. District Court in Detroit to enjoin the Fruehauf board from concluding the management buyout. A preliminary injunction was issued on July 24 along with an order that the board reopen the bidding to permit Edelman to bid on an equal basis with management. Fruehauf appealed.

On August 8, the United States Court of Appeals of the Sixth Circuit generally affirmed the trial court's decree. Fruehauf had a difficult record on which to justify its board's decisions. Several directors had admitted bias in favor of management. While refusing to talk to Edelman, they had agreed to pay $30 million in corporate funds to Merrill Lynch as financing and advisory fees to facilitate the management proposal. They had also made available $100 million of corporate funds for management to purchase shares and had tied their own hands in negotiation of another offer. No effort had been made to get a counteroffer from Edelman. Further, the amendments of Fruehauf's stock option plan, incentive compensation plan, and pension plans constituted a virtually indigestible pill for any rival to swallow. As the trial court had found, "These amendments would make it impossible for an outside bidder to compete on even terms with management bidders."

However, provisions in the trial court order restraining the directors from using corporate funds to effectuate the buyout were found to be overbroad. The proposition that corporate funds could never be used to encourage bidders or to encourage management buyouts was rejected by the Court of Appeals. Expenditures to finance the flow of information were necessary, said Judge Gilbert S. Merritt, as were "advisory fees for lawyers and investment bankers to structure and conduct the bidding process." In some instances — where the board is clearly neutral — commitment fees of bankers could be paid. However, the Court of Appeals affirmed the District Court's conclusion that the board's "largesse in favor of the managers, their bankers and Merrill Lynch was out of proportion."

One of the three appellate judges, Judge Ralph B. Guy, strongly dissented. He thought the board's resistance could have been intended to force a higher tender offer, since the net result was an increased offer from $44 a share to $48.50 a share, more than $20 higher than the trading price before the takeover attempt. Any decision by the board, he said, "involves an evaluation of the upside benefit of getting perhaps a dollar more per share versus the downside of possibly losing the white knight in the process." He thought that the board's calculations, although perhaps "philosophically unpalatable," were within the business judgment rule.

The battle for Fruehauf ended two weeks later. After forty-eight hours of marathon negotiations, management offered a $1.1 billion LBO at $49 per share. Edelman decided to go no higher. "I am disappointed at not getting the company," said Edelman, but "I was tired of the acrimony." However, Edelman may have been partly consoled by the $49 per share price that Merrill Lynch paid him for his 2.1 million shares, a profit of about $30 million, and the additional reimbursement of his $21 million in legal and financial expenses incurred in the struggle.

o o o

In any auction of a company, the law wants to ensure that outside groups are not precluded from bidding on an equal basis. Both the *Revlon* and *SCM* decisions suggest that lockups that preclude competitive bidding cannot legally be granted in the midst of a continuing, active bidding process. As the *Revlon* court made clear, once the board has reached a decision to sell the company and another bidder has appeared, the primary duty of the directors is to maximize value to share-holders. This principle has even greater force when one of the bidders is a management-led group.

The metaphor of a level playing field, however, obscures some serious practical difficulties in the concept. In many potential takeover situations a management buyout is the only feasible alternative to the raider's proposal. This is particularly true when the target company is a conglomerate of substantial size. In such a situation, it is unlikely that a white knight will enter the field. Yet, time pressure may make it difficult or impossible for the target to sell off its own parts in an orderly way. Moreover, this kind of dismemberment can destroy management morale at the divisional level, and obviously such morale is a vital ingredient in the prosperity of a diversified company. A management buyout therefore may be the only competition for the raider.

At this point conflict arises between the concept of treating bidders equally — the level playing field — and the reality of organizing a management LBO. Members of top management of a modern corporation usually are well paid. However, it is unusual for any of them, except for senior officers of long tenure and frugal habits, to have amassed any substantial capital. Certainly it will be atypical for the top managers as a group to have the kind of capital required. Still more unusual will it be for them to have this kind of capital in a ratio among themselves that will reflect the contribution they can make in the successor company. Thus, an incumbent management almost always needs outside financing to put together a proposal that can compete with the raider's proposal.

But putting together financing on the scale required for a leveraged buyout itself takes substantial up-front financing. An investment banker has to be retained to advise about possible financial structure, price proposals, and the "mix" in any offer; to provide necessary bridge financing; and to find additional funding sources. Sometimes more than one investment banker is necessary. High-caliber, expensive legal advice is required, both in shaping a plan and in carrying it out.

Sudden, difficult litigation has to be anticipated and its cost provided for. These preliminary steps can require millions of dollars. Most or all of the money can be provided by the target corporation, with the directors' approval. Yet providing these funds, it could be argued, is a violation of the level-playing-field principle because the funds are used to support a management proposal against the outsider's proposal.

In *Edelman* v. *Fruehauf Corporation,* however, the board completely lost sight of the concept of a level playing field. The Fruehauf board, faced with an unsolicited outsider's offer, made available $100 million in corporate funds to the buyout group led by management. It agreed to pay breakup fees, commitment fees, and the compensation of the group's investment bankers. It refused to negotiate with the hostile bidder, signed a no-shop clause with the management group, enacted a pension parachute, and accelerated employee benefit plans. The Court of Appeals for the Sixth Circuit found that the totality of the board's actions amounted to a rubber stamp of the management proposal.

The court said it was acceptable to pay the lawyers' fees and probably the banking fees. But it imposed a higher burden of justification on commitment fees — fees paid to the lenders as a guarantee that the loan will be made. Commitment fees are essential as a practical matter and can be very substantial — as much as $5 million — and they become due when the LBO agreement is signed. The court in *Edelman* v. *Fruehauf* suggested that these fees can be paid if the board has shown itself to be "unbiased" and "impartial." This may mean that, if the investment banker gives an opinion that the price is fair, the financing is feasible, and the deal can be done, the board may then say "Let's do it." If the deal then goes forward, fair and good.

However, suppose that two weeks later another buyer appears prepared to bid $8 more, with financing lined up, but wants the company to pay his commitment fee. Or suppose that the original outsider raises his bid, and management has to regroup, trying either to cancel the prior commitment fee or to get a new commitment, but in either case having to pay an additional fee. How is the auction to be kept going? The question inevitably arises of whether at that point the company — in order to be evenhanded and impartial — has not undertaken to subsidize the auction process.

Commitment fees are extremely important in LBOs because the acquisition is usually made with very little money down and the rest borrowed. To the extent that restrictions are put on these fees, it is more difficult to effect a management buyout. One solution is for the agreement to provide for the company's paying the financial fees to other bona fide bidders with higher bids. That makes a level playing field, and that keeps the game going.

Perhaps the courts' concern about self-interested transactions by management is best met by having a special committee of outside directors as exclusive representatives of shareholder interests act as the decision-making body, with its own investment bankers and lawyers. Together they become the agents of the shareholders. To guide the special committee along its difficult path, we offer the following rules:

Independent Directors. The decision-making process should be guided by directors who have no interest in the buyout proposal and who, to the extent feasible, have no material financial relationship to the company. The decision-making process itself should be calculated to render an informed decision, consistent with the primary objectives of shareholders. Minutes should reflect the nature and scope of its discussions.

Information. A crucial factor in both the *Van Gorkom* and *SCM* decisions was the neglect of directors in obtaining information necessary to informed decisions. The transgression in *Van Gorkom* was in the court's view particularly egregious, for the board there proceeded without any written analyses. In *SCM*, the independent committee failed to secure information beyond that supplied by SCM's financial adviser and made no inquiries regarding the significance of the information. Information should be obtained from both reliable internal company sources and independent experts. Management should be required to provide financial advisers whatever information they request.

The Role of Advisers. The committee should actively utilize its investment bankers and legal counsel. As stated in the American Law Institute corporate governance project, corporate law permits directors, acting in good faith, to rely

> on information, opinions, reports, or statements, including financial statements and other financial data, if prepared or presented by officers or employees of the corporation whom the director reasonably believes to be competent in the matters presented; legal counsel, public accountants, or other persons as to matters the director reasonably believes are within the person's expert competence.

Deliberation. Within the limits of urgency, the special committee should take the time necessary to evaluate thoroughly all proposals. Courts have recognized that the degree of urgency affects the extent of appropriate deliberations.

Sale or No Sale. In evaluating either an LBO offer or an outside offer, the special committee must make two distinct recommendations to the board: whether to sell the company at all and whether the specific proposal should be accepted or better terms negotiated. Obviously, the extent to which the LBO proposal is acceptable can affect whether the company should be sold. Of the factors to be weighed by the special committee, price and feasibility are the most important.

A Fair Price. In determining what is a fair price, a foremost consideration is whether a present sale is opportune — may the company be worth substantially more later? The measure of valuation is also critical. The following factors are usually paramount: the company's value if sold as a going concern to a third party; its liquidation value; its value in a standard leveraged buyout; and its value on a restructured basis. Traditional measures of value such as book value and premium over market are relevant factors, but courts are increasingly receptive to more sophisticated financial analysis. The Delaware Supreme Court has held that a premium over market price is not by itself indicative that an offered price is fair.

The best approach is to consider whether a particular offer is fair, rather than trying to determine a precise figure at which the special committee would recommend a sale. Financial advisers typically suggest a range of prices that could be considered fair. Whenever possible, the committee or its representatives should seek by negotiation to improve the price and other terms of the proposal.

Feasibility. Will the shareholders actually realize the payoff that a proposal promises? The feasibility of the transaction is affected by the financing, time to consummation, and viability of the surviving entity as a going concern. Whether the company will be undercapitalized or incapable of meeting its contemplated debts as they mature has to be considered. If it is later proved that there were deficiencies in these respects, unpaid creditors or a trustee in bankruptcy may seek to recover payments made to shareholders in the transaction.

Dealings with other potential bidders must be circumspect. Recommending an LBO proposal necessarily implies that the company should be sold. A decision to negotiate with the LBO group, however, does not impose a duty to solicit other offers for the company. Nor is the company precluded from entering into contractual obligations with a bidder to facilitate or induce an acquisition transaction.

Except in unusual circumstances, such as a clearly preemptive offer, the committee should not authorize an option on shares, or on assets, a bust-up fee, or other benefit to a bidder that would effectively prevent competition, unless granting such a benefit occurs *after* a period of soliciting other offers. With this qualification, granting a lockup or bust-up fees may be appropriate, depending upon their cost; their probable deterrent effect on other offers; the extent to which other offers have been solicited; the nature of the financing for the proposed transaction; and the likelihood that the deal will go through. Commitments for substantial expenditures for a management group will be rigorously scrutinized by the courts to see whether the playing field was approximately level.

o   o   o

The New Princes
of Industry

A T THE BEGINNING of the book we noted that the mergers and acquisitions phenomenon, and the resulting
boardroom turmoil, were a ripple on top of a wave on top of
an oceanic flood of powerful changes occurring in the world
economy since the mid-1960s. Political analysts have said that
Pax Americana — a state of world peace supposedly maintained by American arms — began a decline sometime about
then, if not earlier. One could say that *Fisc Americana* — a
world economy dominated by American industry and the dollar — began a decline about the same time or a little later.
And for the same reasons. Other countries were beginning to
catch up.

This change has been extremely painful. It is manifested
in American foreign policy frustrations in such places as Viet-
nam, Lebanon, the Persian Gulf, and Nicaragua. It is reflected in such business frustrations as the foreign invasion
of American markets, particularly of those we invented (for
example, the mass market for automobiles and television sets),
and in such financial concerns as the state of the U.S. dollar.
It has been registered in the October 1987 stock market crash
and felt in the labor market and in industry-based communities. It is felt by management, as most businesses have come
to operate under the pressures and uncertainties once known
only in show business and advertising. And it is felt in the
boardroom, where directors may have to decide whether to
radically restructure a company whose managers are long-

time professional associates and whose policies they have firmly supported. Allegis Corporation is yet another case in point.

On June 9, 1987, at 3:00 P.M., the board of the former UAL, Inc. — renamed Allegis Corporation — met in the Rockefeller Center office of Morgan Stanley & Company, one of its investment bankers. The meeting notice indicated that its purpose was to review antitakeover strategies. The meeting itself lasted for seven hours and took a different turn. The outside directors, led by Charles F. Luce, an eighteen-year veteran of the board and retired chairman of Consolidated Edison Company, took charge. The board, among other things, fired Allegis's CEO, Richard J. Ferris. "It became clear," said Luce, "that the market could not wait for Allegis's concept to prove itself."

The rule that "the business and affairs of . . . [a] corporation . . . shall be managed by or under the direction of a board" gives the directors legal authority to fire the CEO. That power can be exercised without giving reasons and without a hearing, so long as in doing so the board members themselves are not guilty of disloyalty to the corporation. Under common law, as developed in the nineteenth century, not only the CEO but all employees serve at will and can be fired at will. But there are constraints on the firing of most employees. In companies that are unionized, blue-collar employees cannot be fired except for cause and within the framework of established grievance procedure. As a matter of practice, these days a white-collar worker cannot simply be fired by a supervisor — the decision has to be justified. However, there are no such legal constraints on firing corporate top management. In imposing such bureaucratic "capital punishment," no reasons need be given, except such purely formal ones as "disagreement over corporate policy," and there is no judicial review.

Richard Ferris, CEO of Allegis since 1979, had risen through the ranks of UAL's hotel and food service systems. His strategic business plan was to convert United Airlines, the world's largest investor-owned airline, into a full-service travel conglomerate that offered packages of air travel, rental car, and hotel room. Ferris was prepared to forsake short-term profits for what he believed would be long-term market dominance and big returns. In June 1985 he bought Hertz from RCA for $587 million; four months later he paid $750 million for Pan American World Airways' Pacific routes; and in 1986 he bought the Hilton International Company for $980 million.

Before May 1987, Coniston Partners, the raiders in the Gelco case, had accumulated a 13 percent stake in Allegis, when the stock was trading in the range of $50 a share. Coniston proposed to sell the Allegis components and distribute the proceeds to shareholders on the premise that the breakup value of the parts was greater than that of the whole. Coniston, working with Bear Stearns, announced its plan on May 26; two days later, the price of Allegis's stock had jumped more than $8.37 to $57.50. Allegis's directors grew increasingly concerned that Coniston would garner stockholder support sufficient to carry out its plan. As a source close to the board told the *New York Times*, "There was a feeling that they would be kicked out unless they did something." To fend off Coniston, the Allegis board on May 28 considered a recapitalization plan involving $3 billion in new debt to finance a $60 per share special dividend.

The pressure for board action intensified on June 4, when United's airline pilot union emerged as another competing bidder. The pilot union proposal, put together with Lazard Frères as investment adviser, called for selling Hertz and the hotels, giving employees the majority ownership in the United Airlines portion of the company, and paying $70 per share to stockholders. On June 9, the union filed suit, demanding that its $70 offer be put to shareholders alongside Allegis's $60 proposal.

Allegis's plan was less attractive because it involved $3 billion of added debt, which could be paid off only if the company could lower its costs, which would require the cooperation of its unions. That cooperation was unlikely as long as Ferris was in charge. Ferris's tough stand in negotiations with the Air Line Pilots Association in 1985 had led to a twenty-nine-day strike that dragged down earnings and embittered the pilots.

According to Charles Luce, the board, watching the company's stock rise, "thought the market was saying that Allegis was worth more broken up and that the current strategy should be abandoned." Although the outside directors had supported Ferris during the company's acquisition program, they now decided that Ferris was an obstacle to restructuring the company. "There comes a point," said Luce, "where no board can impose its own beliefs over the opposition of the people who elected it." Ferris was replaced by Frank A. Olson, chairman of Allegis's Hertz subsidiary.

Once the board fired Ferris, Coniston Partners, which had been supported by institutional investors, called off its proxy campaign. Allegis withdrew its $60 plan because of the high financing costs. Olson announced that Allegis would sell the Westin and Hilton International chains for an estimated $2.2 billion and the Hertz subsidiary for an estimated $850 million and would change the company's name back to United Airlines. An Allegis spokesman would not discuss how the company would evaluate bids, except to say that "maximizing value is a key factor."

Coniston had dropped its proxy campaign but in the process turned a $520 million investment into a stake worth about $700 million. Paul E. Tierney, Jr., a Coniston general partner, called it a triumph of "strategic block investing — acquiring a large block of stock not to own or run the company but to influence corporate policy."

In October Hilton International was sold for $1.07 billion. In December Allegis sold Hertz Corporation for $1.3 billion to an investment group formed by Ford Motor Company and Hertz senior managers. On February 1, 1988, the Westin Hotels subsidiary was sold to Aoki Corporation of Japan, a Tokyo-based international construction company, and the Robert M. Bass Group for $1.53 billion. With proceeds from sales of the hotel and car rental operations, in mid-February 1988 the company began an $80 cash self-tender for approximately two thirds of its shares.

o o o

Where does control in the American corporation now lie? Adolph Berle and Gardiner Means may have been correct fifty years ago when they said that management controls the modern corporation. But, as the Allegis restructuring shows, control is now a troika: management, which controls operations; stockholders, who exercise continuous pressure through their rights of ownership; and market-sensitive directors, who continually reevaluate company health. This represents a major shift in the balance of power within the corporation in favor of the board.

The change in the board's power position results from a combination of two factors, one legal and the other financial and economic. Legally, the board's traditional formal authority regarding mergers and acquisitions has simply remained intact. The significant legal happening with regard to the legal power of the board is that nothing has happened.

Although management can favor a merger, as in the *Van Gorkom* case, or recommend against it, as in *Unocal* and *Revlon,* management still cannot proceed without the board because legally the board has the power of decision. *De jure* — the legal phrase meaning "under the law" — the board has final judgment. As shown in *Charitable Corporation* v. *Sutton,* a corporation's board of directors has always had that power *de jure.* But now that formal power is also power *de facto,* and it is reinforced by the prospect of litigation, where the directors will have to demonstrate that they personally studied, understood, and approved the action.

Since the directors always have had ultimate legal responsibility, even when they were merely parsley on the fish, the law has not fundamentally changed. Then what has?

The change has been in the circumstances in which directors now must carry out those responsibilities. A legal rule that is unchanged in its terms can have very different practi-

cal significance if there is change in the circumstances in
which it applies. The fifty-five-mile-an-hour speed limit means
one thing when there is a consensus favoring gasoline con-
servation and serious enforcement of speed limits; it means
quite another thing when there is no such consensus. The
effective level of our fifty-five-mile-an-hour speed limit has now
become seventy miles an hour, as every truck driver knows.

Financial and economic changes similarly have altered the
effective significance of corporate-governance law. Twenty
years ago, mergers were friendly matters between gentlemen,
and hostile takeovers were virtually unheard of. The likelihood of a takeover was roughly the same as the possibility in
the days of gunboat diplomacy that some second-rate foreign
regime might try to expropriate American property or even
take American citizens as hostages. Just as the risks of such
revolutionary politics have become a fact of life in international corporate affairs, so also the risks of unfriendly takeovers have become a fact of life in domestic corporate affairs.
The possibility of merger or acquisition is now a specter constantly hovering over every major corporation. A kind of business risk that only the board of directors has authority to deal
with has become a part of the normal existence of the American business corporation.

In effect, boards themselves now compete in the marketplace. Every company is a potential target, and every target
has to enhance value to its shareholders. That responsibility
ultimately rests with the directors, and outside directors play
a key role. The only recourse from the board is the courts, but
the courts accord basic deference to the directors' judgment.

The market price of a company's stock no longer can be
assumed to represent its fair value. If a tender offer appears
unfair, *Unocal* v. *Mesa Petroleum* permits the board to block
it with means appropriate to the threat. *Gelco Corporation* v.
Coniston Partners permits the board to restructure the company, but the *Revlon* decision requires the board to sell the
company to the highest bidder once a decision to sell has been
made. In making these strategic decisions, the directors ob-

tain the benefits and protections of the business judgment rule. Whatever shades of meaning are given to the business judgment rule, the courts recognize that the judgment call in a takeover or restructuring is basically that of the directors.

However, the courts can second-guess the directors. There is no longer an unquestioning presumption that a board has performed its responsibility. The turning point was *Unocal*, which led to *Gelco* and *Revlon*. These cases say that a defensive tactic adopted by a board must have a reasonable relationship to the threat posed. A court's holding that a tactic is reasonable is a substantive judgment on the part of the court; it *is* a second guess. To a novel but uncertain extent, therefore, the directors are now subject to judicial reversal of their decisions. In this respect, the law has moved marginally but perceptibly.

Concurrently, there is also movement limiting the potential personal liability for damages to which directors are exposed. This movement is expressed in legislation that modifies the rule, going all the way back to *Charitable Corporation* v. *Sutton*, whereby directors can be liable in damages for breach of the duty of care. Modifications of this rule have been adopted in several states, including Pennsylvania, Ohio, and, of greatest practical importance, Delaware and New York. These statutes in effect insulate a director who is not utterly reckless in performing his responsibilities and who stands to gain nothing personally, which is virtually always the case for an outside director in a takeover situation.

It has been feared that such insulation from liability weakens directors' accountability. There are other influences, however, that constrain directors in the direction of careful exercise of their responsibilities. The directors of a publicly held company understand that they are always the subject of public scrutiny through disclosure; that they can be removed by the shareholders; that they can be liable in damages for reckless misconduct. Most directors are prudent persons with a sense of duty. Whatever the boardroom ethos may once have been, it is now one of care, inquiry, and diligence. Nevertheless, critics believe these legislative changes have weakened directors' accountability, and this sentiment could translate into intercession at the federal level.

The other part of the movement to limit directors' liability is to clarify the rules governing the standard of care itself, a task undertaken in the American Law Institute project on corporate governance. The ALI is a private organization of judges, lawyers, and law professors that reexamines various areas of law to recommend clarification and modernization. Its project on corporate governance has studied such specific areas as the stockholders' derivative suit and the standard of care for directors. This project has generated a great deal of controversy. Whatever else, however, the project has made clear that directors have the benefit of a broadly protective business judgment rule, that they may rely heavily on reports of financial and legal experts in reaching decisions, and that their exposure to damages liability should be circumscribed.

There is emerging a legal distinction that is both obvious and long overdue. The distinction is between the circumstances in which a decision by the directors may be nullified by a court through an injunction, and the circumstances in which the directors may be held liable in damages for having made the decision. The emergent law is that in certain circumstances the courts may second-guess the directors to the extent of setting aside their action concerning the corporation. But damages liability will be imposed only in cases where the directors personally benefited or were guilty of extreme neglect of their responsibility.

Not surprisingly, corporate CEOs feel deep anger and frustration about the takeover movement and the redistribution of power within the corporate structure. Top corporate managers usually have arrived where they are through long years of high-energy devotion to their companies. They know the company's strategic prospects and financial position at least as well as any of the outside directors. They usually understand the inner workings of their businesses better than an outside raider. They have concerns for the stockholders, particularly long-term individual stockholders, that go beyond short-run economics. They have concerns for loyal employees, whose bodies after all are the "fat" that is to be "cut out." They have concerns for the communities that will be left with empty factories when a raider has finished "improving the fit" or with darkened concert halls because of loss of corporate support.

That some stranger playing with a computer and junk bonds can take all that away may be too much to bear for a person who has made the company his life's work and his virtual alter ego. Fred Hartley of Unocal said it all: "We did the best we could in a society that's lost its morality and ethics. Our shareholders didn't get hurt, our employees' position was preserved, our ability to serve our customers continued and the company remained intact."

Has caring management at the corporate helm given way to boards of directors whose concerns are exclusively short-term and numbers-driven? Every corporation now spends time worrying about takeovers that could be well spent worrying about productive efficiency, export markets, and keeping abreast of the Japanese and Germans. Whether a takeover attempt is successful (as in the case of Revlon) or not (as in the case of Union Carbide), the target company usually emerges highly leveraged. Even defensive leveraging results in the cannibalization of American companies that Hartley criticized — companies consuming themselves by buying in their stock. Over the last ten years, companies have bought more of their own stock than they have raised in equity.

When equity has been replaced by debt, stocks go down faster in a bear market. During the crash of 1987, the Dow Jones index dropped from 2700 on August 17 to 1800 ten weeks later. Stocks selling at twenty times earnings on October 16 sold at twelve times earnings on October 20. More than $1 trillion of financial assets was taken out of the economy. Junk bonds, the necessary financing of many takeover attempts, were impossible to sell in the weeks following.

The past possibility and recent actuality of such upheaval

is one factor that underlies public concern over the regulation
of takeover attempts. Congress has adopted tax legislation that
would retard takeovers and is considering amendments to the
securities laws to the same end. Key state legislatures have
already adopted antitakeover legislation. Some observers con-
clude that the cumulative effect of takeovers is a weakening
of American economic strength and our competitive position
in the world. This conclusion would be sound if all or most
takeovers involved prices that were too high, leverage that was
too great, excessive distraction and demoralization of top
management, and pure waste in banker and lawyer fees. On
that premise, it would also be true that any given takeover is
likely to be a mistake. Yet takeovers continue even after the
crash of 1987.

Corporate enterprises are now leaner operations. Sizing down
began in the late 1970s and has intensified in the highly competitive marketplace of the 1980s. Companies lay off not only
blue-collar workers but white-collar ones and management all
the way to the top. Restructuring goes on in companies such
as IBM, Kodak, and Xerox.

Directors must constantly be asking themselves such questions as: Should we be deconglomerating? How can we ra-
tionalize our operations? They must continually reassess the
value of each division of their company. Driven by their accountability to shareholders and the company's exposure to
raiders, directors must make the company more efficient, more
productive, and better valued in the marketplace.

Directors nevertheless must consider also the impact of a
takeover on other constituencies of the corporation. Some
companies have amended their charters expressly to allow
consideration of nonfinancial factors. For example, in November 1986 the shareholders of GTE Corporation ratified a charter
amendment to permit the board to consider the "social, legal,
environmental and economic effects of the acquisition on employees, customers, suppliers and other constituencies of GTE
and its subsidiaries and geographical areas in which GTE and
its subsidiaries . . . are located . . . [and] such other factors

as it deems relevant." Certain states' statutes, including those of Ohio and Pennsylvania, expressly authorize directors to take nonfinancial factors into account in evaluating an acquisition proposal. However, absent legislation or a charter provision like GTE's, the directors' focus must be on the maximization of shareholder value.

Directors, shareholders, and management know that the one constant in the economy is change. But directors know also that their accountability to shareholders reaches back to eighteenth-century legal standards still being adapted to today's realities. The new princes of industry must be careful, methodical, thorough, critical, responsible, and, above all, accountable to shareholders. It is expected. It is demanded by the free market. And it is the law.

o   o   o

Appendix
Boards of Directors

The appendix represents, to the extent possible, the boards of directors at the time of the transactions discussed in the book. The information is gathered from disclosure documents — 10-K's, annual reports to shareholders, and proxy statements for the relevant time periods — as well as from standard corporate and financial references.

An asterisk (*) preceding a name means that the individual served as an outside director.

NAME	AGE	TITLE & OTHER BOARD MEMBERSHIPS	YEAR ELECTED DIRECTOR
TRANS UNION CORPORATION — 1980			
Sidney H. Bonser	56	Executive vice president, Trans Union Corp.	1969
William B. Browder	64	Senior vice president, law, Trans Union Corp.	1954
Bruce S. Chelberg	46	President and chief operating officer, Trans Union Corp.	1978
*William B. Johnson	61	Chairman of the board and chief executive officer, IC Industries, Inc.; director, Abex Corp., Aetna Life Insurance Co., Association of Southeastern Railroads, Chicago Central Area Committee, Continental Illinois Corp.,	1969

NAME	AGE	TITLE & OTHER BOARD MEMBERSHIPS	YEAR ELECTED DIRECTOR
		Continental Illinois National Bank and Trust Co. of Chicago, Illinois Central Gulf Railroad, Pepsi Cola General Bottlers, Pet Inc., Swift & Co., Transportation Association of America; trustee, Committee for Economic Development, Michael Reese Hospital, and Museum of Science and Industry, Chicago	
*Joseph B. Lanterman	65	Retired chairman of the board, Amsted Industries Inc.; director, A. E. Staley Manufacturing Co., American Motorists Insurance Co., Harris Trust and Savings Bank, Illinois Bell Telephone Co., Illinois Central Gulf Railroad, International Harvester Co., Kemper Corp., Lumbermen's Mutual Casualty Co., and Peoples Energy Corp.	1978
*Graham J. Morgan	63	Chairman of the board and chief executive officer, U.S. Gypsum Co.; director, American Hospital Supply Corp., BPB Industries, Illinois Gulf Central Railroad, and International Harvester Co.; member, advisory board of Kemper Insurance Co.	1979
Thomas P. O'Boyle	60	Senior vice president, administration, Trans Union Corp.	1968
*Robert W. Reneker	68	Retired chairman of the board, Esmark Inc.; member, National Executive Board for Boy Scouts of America; director, American Management	1971

NAME	AGE	TITLE & OTHER BOARD MEMBERSHIPS	YEAR ELECTED DIRECTOR
		Association, Community Fund of Chicago, Inc.,Continental Illinois Corp., Continental Illinois National Bank and Trust Co. of Chicago, Grocery Manufacturers of America, John Crerar Library, Lawter Chemicals, Inc., and Morton Norwich Products, Inc; vice chairman, National Alliance of Businessmen Chicago Metro Area; trustee, Farm Foundation, Illinois College of Jacksonville, Museum of Science and Industry, Chicago, and Nutrition Foundation.	
Jerome W. Van Gorkom	63	Chairman of the board and chief executive officer, Trans Union Corp.; director, Champion International Corp., IC Industries, Inc., Illinois Central Gulf Railroad, Lyric Opera of Chicago, and Schering-Plough Corp.	1957
*W. Allen Wallis	68	Chancellor, University of Rochester; director, Bausch and Lomb, Inc., Eastman Kodak Co., Esmark Inc., Lincoln First Bank Rochester, Macmillan, Inc., Metropolitan Life Insurance Co., Rochester Telephone Corp., and Standard Oil Co.	1962

HOUSEHOLD INTERNATIONAL, INC. — 1984

Bernard F. Brennan	46	President and chief executive officer, Household Merchandising, Inc.	1984
Donald C. Clark	53	Chairman of the board and chief executive offi-	1948

NAME	AGE	TITLE & OTHER BOARD MEMBERSHIPS	YEAR ELECTED DIRECTOR
		cer, Household International, Inc.; director, Square D Company, Warner Lambert	1984
Gary G. Dillon	50	President and chief executive officer, Household Manufacturing, Inc.	1984
*Mary Johnston Evans	55	Director, American Hospital Supply Corp., Certain Teed Corp., Delta Air Lines, Inc., and Sun Company, Inc.; member, advisory board of Morgan Stanley & Co.; trustee, Scudder-AARP Growth Trust and Scudder-AARP Insured Tax-Free Income Trust	1977
*Thomas D. Flynn	72	Retired partner, Arthur Young & Co.	1974
William D. Hendry	63	President, Household Finance Corp.; director, Handschy Industries, Inc.	1979
Joseph W. James	58	Executive vice president, Household International, Inc.	1974
*Mitchell P. Kartalia	71	Retired chairman and chief executive officer, Square D Company; director, Rexnord Inc.	1972
*John A. Moran	53	President, Dyson-Kissner-Moran Corp. and MMD Holding Corp.; chairman of the board, Varlin Corp.; director, American National Resources Co. and Northeast Ohio Axle, Inc.	1981
*Gordon P. Osler	62	Chairman of the board, Stanton Pipes Ltd., Transcanada Pipelines Ltd.; chairman and director, Canadian Surety Co. and Slater Steel Industries; director, Maclean-Hunter	1972

NAME	AGE	TITLE & OTHER BOARD MEMBERSHIPS	YEAR ELECTED DIRECTOR
*Arthur E. Rasmussen	62	Ltd., Toronto Dominion Bank, and Uniroyal Ltd. Director, Abbott Laboratories, Central and South West Corp., and Standard Oil Co. (Indiana)	1967
George W. Rauch	65	President and director, Burch Co.; counsel, Chapman and Cutler, Chicago	1967
James M. Tait	64	Retired chairman, Household Merchandising, Inc.; director, Snap-On Tools Corp.	1971
*Raymond C. Tower	60	Director, president, and chief operating officer, FMC Corp.; director, Firestone Tire and Rubber Co.; trustee of five investment trusts designed for institutional investors under the common management of Goldman, Sachs & Co.	1984
*Miller Upton	68	Past president, Beloit College; director, American Capital Bond Fund, American Capital Convertible Securities, Inc., American General Series Portfolio Co., and Home Life Insurance Co. of New York	1965
John C. Whitehead	62	Co-chairman and senior partner, Goldman, Sachs & Co.; director, American District Telegraph Co., Crompton Co., Inc., Crompton & Knowles Corp., Dillard Department Stores, Inc., Loctite Corp., and Pillsbury Co.	1970

UNOCAL CORPORATION — 1984

NAME	AGE	TITLE & OTHER BOARD MEMBERSHIPS	YEAR ELECTED DIRECTOR
*William F. Ballhaus	66	Retired president and chief executive officer,	1977

NAME	AGE	TITLE & OTHER BOARD MEMBERSHIPS	YEAR ELECTED DIRECTOR
		Beekman Instruments, Inc.; director, Northrop Corp. and Republic Automotive Parts, Inc.	
Claude S. Brinegar	58	Senior vice president, administration, Unocal Corp.	1968
Ray A. Burke	63	Senior vice president, energy resources, Unocal Corp.	1966
*Robert D. Campbell	67	Retired chairman of the board, Newsweek Inc.	1981
*William H. Doheny	66	Personal investments	1954
Richard K. Eamer	57	Chairman of the board and chief executive officer, National Medical Enterprises, Inc.; director, Imperial Bank	1981
*Lewis B. Harder	66	Vice president and chairman of the board, Pacific Holding Corp.; director, Bancroft Convertible Fund, Inc., Brascan Ltd., Danaher Corp., Flexi-Van Corp., Madison Resources, Inc., Marmon Group, Inc., and Pittsburgh & West Virginia Railroad; president and chairman of the board, International Mining Corp., a subsidiary of Pacific Holding Corp.	1977
Fred L. Hartley	68	Chairman of the board, president, and principal executive officer, Unocal Corp.; director, International Speedway Corp., Rockwell International, and Union Banks; member, American Chemical Society; trustee, California Institute of Technology and U.S. Council of the International Chamber of Commerce, Inc.	1960

NAME	AGE	TITLE & OTHER BOARD MEMBERSHIPS	YEAR ELECTED DIRECTOR
T. C. Henderson	64	Senior vice president, Unocal Corp., president, Union Chemicals Division	1976
*Donald P. Jacobs	57	Dean, J. L. Kellogg Graduate School of Management, Northwestern University; director, Commonwealth Edison Co., First Chicago Corp., First National Bank of Chicago, Galaxy Carpet Mills, Inc., Hartmarx Corp., Swift Independent Corp., and Universal Development Corp.	1972
William S. McConnor	65	Senior vice president, Unocal Corp., and president, Union 76 Division	1973
*Peter O'Malley	47	President, Los Angeles Dodgers, Inc.; director of Bank America Corp.	1976
Richard J. Stegemeier	56	Senior vice president, corporate development, Unocal Corp.; member, American Petroleum Institute, Society of Petroleum Engineers, and World Petroleum Congress	1980
*Donn B. Tatum	71	Chairman, Executive Committee, Walt Disney Productions	1977

UNION CARBIDE CORPORATION — 1985

NAME	AGE	TITLE & OTHER BOARD MEMBERSHIPS	YEAR ELECTED DIRECTOR
Warren M. Anderson	64	Chairman of the board and chief executive officer, Union Carbide Corp.; director, Aetna Life & Casualty Co., Sonat Inc., Southern Natural Gas Co., and Ucar Capital Corp., a subsidiary of Union Carbide; member, Business Council, Business Roundtable, and National Energy Foundation	1974

NAME	AGE	TITLE & OTHER BOARD MEMBERSHIPS	YEAR ELECTED DIRECTOR
*R. Manning Brown, Jr.	69	Passed away in October 1985; chairman of the board and chief executive officer, New York Life Insurance Co.; director, Associated Dry Goods Corp., Avon Products Inc., J. P. Morgan & Co., Inc., and Union Camp Corp.	1970
*John J. Creedon	61	Director, president, and chief executive officer, Metropolitan Life Insurance Co.; director, Albany Life Assurance Co. Ltd., Melville Corp., NYNEX Corp., and State Street Research & Management Corp.	1984
Alec Flamm	58	President and chief operating officer, Union Carbide Corp.; vice chairman of the board and director, Continental Corp.	1981
*Harry J. Gray	66	Chairman of the board and chief executive officer, United Technologies Corp.; director, Citicorp, Citibank N.A., and Council for the United States and Italy; chairman of the board, National Science Center for Communications and Electronics Foundation; member, Conference Board, Council on Foreign Relations, Navy League of the United States, and President's National Security Telecommunications Advisory Committee	1981
*James M. Hester	61	President, New York Botanical Garden; director, Robert Lehman Foundation Inc., Harry Frank Guggenheim Foundation;	1963

NAME	AGE	TITLE & OTHER BOARD MEMBERSHIPS	YEAR ELECTED DIRECTOR
		trustee, United Board for Higher Christian Education in Asia	
*Jack B. Jackson	69	Retired president of J. C. Penney Co.; director of various other corporations and organizations	1974
*Horace C. Jones	69	Director, Beneficial Mutual Savings Bank of Philadelphia, Burlington Industries, Inc., and Russell Reynolds Associates, Inc; trustee, Chestnut Hill Hospital, Philadelphia	1976
Robert D. Kennedy	53	President, Chemical and Plastics Group, Union Carbide Corp.; director, Union Carbide Canada Ltd.; member, Executive Committee of the Board, Chemical Manufacturers Association	July 1985
*Ronald L. Kuehn, Jr.	50	Director, chief executive officer, and president, Sonat Inc.; director, AM-South Bancorporation and various subsidiaries of Sonat Inc.	1984
*C. Peter McColough	63	Director, Business Council, Citicorp, Citibank N.A., Council on Foreign Relations, Knight-Ridder Newspapers, Inc., and Xerox Corp.; trustee, University of Rochester	1979
*William S. Sneath	59	Retired chairman of the board and chief executive officer, Union Carbide Corp.; director, American District Telegraph Co., Barclays International Ltd., JWT Group, Inc., Metropolitan Life Insurance Co., and Rockwell International Corp.; mem-	1969

NAME	AGE	TITLE & OTHER BOARD MEMBERSHIPS	YEAR ELECTED DIRECTOR
		ber, Business Council and Conference Board; trustee, Williams College	
Heinn F. Tomfohrde III	52	President, Consumer and Industrial Products and Service groups, Union Carbide Corp.; trustee, Trinity Liquid Assets Mutual Fund	1985
*Roberto de Jesus Toro	37	Director and chairman, Executive Committee, Banco de Ponce; director, Puerto Rican American Corp. and Puerto Rican Cement Co., Inc.	1971
*Russell E. Train	65	Chairman, World Wildlife Fund–U.S.; director and chairman, Conservation Foundation; trustee, Rockefeller Brothers Fund, Scientists Institute for Public Information, and World Resources for the Future	1977 1977
*Kathryn D. Wriston	46	Director, Federated Department Stores, Inc., Santa Fe Southern Pacific Corp., and various other corporations and organizations	1977

GELCO CORPORATION — 1986

NAME	AGE	TITLE & OTHER BOARD MEMBERSHIPS	YEAR ELECTED DIRECTOR
*Samuel D. Addoms	47	Chairman of the board, Addoms & Humphrey Business Development	1977
*Jack J. Crocker	62	Consultant, Gelco Corp.; director, Data Card Corp., Ecolab Inc., Piper, Jaffray and Hopwood, Inc., Scott Paper Co., and United Stationers, Inc.	1978
*Jaye F. Dyer	59	Director, president, and chief executive officer, Dyco Petroleum Corp.; director, Diversified Ener-	1969

NAME	AGE	TITLE & OTHER BOARD MEMBERSHIPS	YEAR ELECTED DIRECTOR
		gies, Inc., and Northwestern National Life Insurance Co.	
*William F. Foss	69	Consultant, Gelco Corp.; director, Apache Corp. and Applied Power, Inc.	1969
*Neil Goldschmidt	45	Vice president, Nike International, Inc.; director, National Semiconductor, Inc.; resigned in January 1987 and became governor-elect, state of Oregon	1982
Andrew C. Grossman	35	Executive vice president, Gelco Corp.	1983
*Harold I. Grossman	60	President, Forgals Financial Inc.	1957
N. "Bud" Grossman	65	Chairman of the board and chief executive officer, Gelco Corp.; director, Ecolab Inc., General Mills, Inc., Northern States Power Co., Northwest Corp., Norwest Bank Minneapolis, N.A., and Toro Co.	1957
Richard W. McFerran	49	Executive vice president and chief financial officer, Gelco Corp.	1986
M. D. McVay	68	President, livestock production, McVay Cos.; chairman of the board, Midwest Inc.	1985
Michael J. Morris	51	Executive vice president, Gelco Corp.; president, Gelco Building and Trailer Services	1975
*Sam Singer	70	Consultant, Gelco Corp.	1969
*Clarence W. Spangle	61	Consultant, Gelco Corp.; director, Lee Data Corp., MAI/Basic Four Co., MSA, Inc., and Silvar-Lisco Inc.	1977
*Mark H. Willes	45	President, General Mills, Inc.; director, General Mills, Inc., and Toro Co.	1981

NAME	AGE	TITLE & OTHER BOARD MEMBERSHIPS	YEAR ELECTED DIRECTOR

REVLON, INC. — 1984

NAME	AGE	TITLE & OTHER BOARD MEMBERSHIPS	YEAR ELECTED DIRECTOR
*Simon Aldewereld	75	Former consultant and general partner, Lazard Frères & Co.; former vice president of finance, World Bank	1976
Sander P. Alexander	55	Senior vice president, finance, and chief financial officer, Revlon, Inc.	1977
Jay I. Bennett	59	Senior vice president, personnel and industrial relations, Revlon Inc.; member, American Arbitration Association, American Management Association, National Association of Manufacturers, and National Industrial Conference Board	1974
Michel C. Bergerac	53	Chairman of the board, president, and chief executive officer, Revlon, Inc.; director, CBS Inc. and Manufacturers Hanover Corp.; member, Board of Overseers, Cornell Medical School	1974
Irving J. Bottner	69	Senior vice president, Revlon, Inc.; president and director, Revlon Professional Products Group; president, Revlon Haircolor, Inc.; director, State Beauty Supply Co.; chairman, Rowx Laboratories, Inc., and General Wig Manufacturers, Inc.	1956
*Jacob Burns	83	Attorney at law; director, Benjamin Cardozo School of Law; honorary trustee, George Washington University	1966
*Lewis L. Glucksman	59	Executive vice president, Fireman's Fund Insur-	1983

NAME	AGE	TITLE & OTHER BOARD MEMBERSHIPS	YEAR ELECTED DIRECTOR
		ance Cos., a subsidiary of American Express Co.; chairman of the board and chief executive officer, Lehman Brothers Kuhn Loeb Inc. from January 1984 to November 1984; commissioner and chairman, Finance Committee, Port Authority of New York and New Jersey	
*John Loudon	49	Managing director, overseas operations, and member, Management and Executive committees, N. M. Rothschild & Sons Ltd., London; director, Heineken, N.V., the Netherlands	1983
*Aileen Mehle	60	Syndicated columnist Suzy Knickerbocker	1972
*Simon H. Rifkind	83	Partner, Paul, Weiss, Rifkind, Wharton & Garrison; director, MacAndrews & Forbes Holdings, Inc., and Sterling Bancorp	1956
Samuel L. Simmons	55	Senior vice president and general counsel, Revlon, Inc.	1976
*Ian R. Wilson	55	Investment consultant; president, chief executive officer and director, Castle & Cooke, Inc., from March 1983 to December 1984; director, Crown Zellerbach Corp.	1984
Paul P. Woolard	61	Senior executive vice president, Revlon, Inc.; president, Revlon Beauty Group; director, Lynch Corp.	1986
*Ezra K. Zilkha	59	President and director, Zilkha & Sons, Inc., and Zilkha Corp.; director,	1981

NAME	AGE	TITLE & OTHER BOARD MEMBERSHIPS	YEAR ELECTED DIRECTOR
		Chicago Milwaukee Corp., CIGNA Corp., Handy & Harman, and Newhall Land & Farming Co.	

SCM CORPORATION — 1985

NAME	AGE	TITLE & OTHER BOARD MEMBERSHIPS	YEAR ELECTED DIRECTOR
*Robert O. Bass	68	Director, Raymond Corp.; retired director, Borg-Warner Corp.; trustee, Field Museum of Natural History	1975
*Robert P. Bauman	54	Vice chairman, Textron, Inc.; chairman of the board and chief executive officer, Avco Corp.; director, Capital Cities Communication Inc., McKesson Corp., and Palm Beach Inc.; trustee, Ohio Wesleyan University and Spelman College	1982
*John T. Booth	55	Chairman of the board, American Health Capital, Inc.; director, VHA Enterprises, Inc.; trustee, New York Society Library; vestryman, Trinity Church, New York City	1965
Paul H. Elicker	62	Chairman of the board and chief executive officer, SCM Corp.; director, Transway International Corp.; vice chairman of the board of trustees, American Management Association; trustee, Archaeological Institute of America	1964
George E. Hall	59	Senior vice president, administration, SCM Corp.	1965
D. George Harris	52	President and chief operating officer, SCM Corp.; director, Chemical Manufacturers Association	July 1985
*Crocker Nevin	62	Senior adviser, Drexel Burnham Lambert, Inc.;	1967

NAME	AGE	TITLE & OTHER BOARD MEMBERSHIPS	YEAR ELECTED DIRECTOR
		chairman of the board, CF&I Steel Corporation; director, ACCION International, BOC Group, Constitution Reinsurance Co., International Insurance Co., Medco Containment Services, Inc., North River Insurance Co., PLC, U.S. Fire Insurance Co., and Westchester Insurance Co.; trustee, Education Broadcasting Corp.	
*Charles W. Parry	61	Chairman of the board and chief executive officer, Aluminum Co. of America; director, First Interstate Bancorp; trustee, Carnegie-Mellon University and Carlow College	1982
*Thomas G. Pownall	63	Chairman of the board and chief executive officer, Martin Marietta Corp.; director, Sunstrand Corp. and Mellon Stuart Co.; trustee, GEICO Investment Series Trust and GEICO Tax Advantage Series Trust	1983
*E. Everett Smith	72	Executive adviser to the profit sharing plan of McKinsey & Company, Inc.; director, Greenwich Research Associates and Trust Corp.; trustee, United States Trust Co. of New York; chairman emeritus, Lenox Hill Hospital	1973
*David W. Wallace	61	Chairman of the board, FECO Engineering Systems, Inc.; director, AE Capital Corp., Eastern Airlines, Lone Star Indus-	1982

NAME	AGE	TITLE & OTHER BOARD MEMBERSHIPS	YEAR ELECTED DIRECTOR
		tries, several mutual funds of the National Securities and Research Corp., and Todd Shipyards; trustee, Smith College; member, Board of Governors, New York Hospital; president, Robert R. Young Foundation	
*Richard R. West	47	Dean, Graduate School of Business, New York University; director, Addison-Wesley Publishing Co., Alexander's Inc., Dorsey Corp., Merrill Lynch Corporate and Municipal Bond Funds, Merrill Lynch Fund for Tomorrow, Merrill Lynch International Holdings, Inc., Sci/Tech Holdings, Inc., and Vornado, Inc.; trustee, CMA Government, Money and Tax-Exempt Trusts	1982

FRUEHAUF CORPORATION — 1984

NAME	AGE	TITLE & OTHER BOARD MEMBERSHIPS	YEAR ELECTED DIRECTOR
*Jack Breslin	64	Vice president, administration and public affairs, and professor, Michigan State University; director, Bank of Lansing and Jackson National Life Insurance Co.	1975
*Donald Chamberlin	48	President, Asset Timing Corp.	1972
Frank P. Coyer, Jr.	65	Vice chairman, finance and administration, Fruehauf Corp.	1973
*John P. Grace	36	President, John P. Grace & Co.; director, Texas Commerce Bank	1981
Russell G. Howell	60	Executive vice president, financial affairs, Fruehauf Corp.; chairman, Frue-	1980

NAME	AGE	TITLE & OTHER BOARD MEMBERSHIPS	YEAR ELECTED DIRECTOR
		hauf Finance Co.; director, McLouth Steel Corp.; member, American Trucking Association and National Accounting and Finance Council	
*John C. McCabe	61	Chief executive officer and chief administrative officer, Blue Cross and Blue Shield of Michigan; chairman, Board of Directors, Blue Cross and Blue Shield Association	1985
Thomas J. Reghanti	60	President and chief operating officer, Fruehauf Corp.; chairman and president, Fruehauf Canada, Inc.	1976
*Dean E. Richardson	57	Chairman of the board and chief executive officer, Manufacturers National Bank of Detroit and Manufacturers National Corp.; president, Manufacturers National Corp.; director, Detroit Edison Co., R. P. Scherer Corp., and Tecumseh Products Co.	1980
Robert D. Rowan	63	Chairman of the board and chief executive officer, Fruehauf Corp.; director, Fruehauf Finance Co. and Fruehauf de Mexico, S.A.; vice president and director, Fruehauf International Ltd.	1970
John D. Schapiro	71	Chairman of the board, Jacksonville Shipyards, Inc., subsidiary of Fruehauf Corp.; chairman, Boston Metals Co.; member, National Executive Board for Boy Scouts of America; trustee, Maryland Historical Society	1980

NAME	AGE	TITLE & OTHER BOARD MEMBERSHIPS	YEAR ELECTED DIRECTOR
Frances Sehn	66	Chairman of the board, Comau Productivity Systems Inc.; chief executive officer, Fran Sehn Co.; life fellow, Institute of Production Engineers; member, Institute of Directors, London; trustee, St. Mary's College	1980
James S. Wilkerson	64	Retired executive vice president, automotive operations, Fruehauf Corp.; chairman of the board and chief executive officer, Kelsey-Hayes Co., a subsidiary of Fruehauf Corp.	1977

o   o   o

Notes

The Parsley on the Fish

Adolph Berle and Gardiner Means, *The Modern Corporation and Private Property*, New York: Commerce Clearing House, 1932.

Alexis de Tocqueville, *Democracy in America*, J. P. Mayer, ed., New York: Harper & Row, 1966, p. 248.

John Kenneth Galbraith, *The Great Crash, 1929*, Cambridge: Riverside Press, 1954.

PROLOGUE:
Nine Honorable Men

Throughout the book, facts and quotes not otherwise documented in the Notes are from the decisions of the court in the case discussed.

The Prologue is based on the Delaware Supreme Court case Smith v. Van Gorkom, 488 A.2d 858 (Del. 1985). Many facts were taken from the Proxy Statement, January 19, 1981, and Supplement to Proxy Statement, January 26, 1981.

Jerome Van Gorkom's public offices: *Chicago Tribune*, December 9, 16, 17, and 21, 1979.

Members of Trans Union's board: Annual Report, 1980. See also Appendix.

Trans Union Corporation: Annual Report, 1980; *New York Times*, February 26, 1984.

Jay Pritzker and the Marmon Group, Inc.: "The Latest Pritzker Bid Is the Most Ambitious," *Business Week*, October 6, 1980, 38. Ira Harris on Jay Pritzker's reputation as a deal maker: *New York Times*, February 26, 1984.

On September 22, 1980, according to the *New York Times*, news of Marmon's bid sent the price of Trans Union's stock up 14½ points; Marmon picking up a "very solid company": *New York Times*, September 23, 1980.

Testimony of Van Gorkom's meeting with Jack Kruizenga after announcement of the merger: Deposition of Van Gorkom, taken January 19, 1981, at Trans Union's headquarters in Chicago, in Alden Smith v. Jay A. Pritzker, et al., Delaware Chancery Court, 8 Del. J. Corp. L. 406, July 6, 1982. Jay

Pritzker subsequently was dismissed from the case; hence the citation of the Delaware Supreme Court case *Smith* v. *Van Gorkom,* the next defendant's name on the list.

Henry Kravis's written notice in early October 1980 of KKR's interest: *Wall Street Journal,* April 11, 1986.

Van Gorkom's concern about the conflict of interest in an LBO: Deposition of Van Gorkom, January 19, 1981.

Threat of Plaintiff's attorney, William Prickett, a partner of Prickett, Jones, Elliott, Kristol & Schnee of Wilmington, Delaware, to take the case to the Delaware Supreme Court: *Chicago Tribune,* February 11, 1981.

Bruce Chelberg, Kruizenga, and Van Gorkom after the merger: *New York Times,* September 15, 1982.

Pritzker's bailout of nine directors of Trans Union: *New York Times,* December 15, 1985. Also see Dennis J. Block, Nancy E. Barton, and Stephen A. Radin, *The Business Judgment Rule,* New Jersey: Prentice Hall Law & Business, 1987, p. 38, footnote 69.

The aftermath of the Trans Union deal for the Pritzkers: *New York Times,* February 26, 1986.

Justice Robert Jackson's comment on courts and judges: Brown v. Allen, 344 U.S. 443 (1953).

CHAPTER 1.
"To Direct and Superintend the Affairs of the Corporation."

Samuel Johnson's quote, ". . . rich beyond the dreams of avarice": James Boswell, *Life of Johnson,* ed. G. B. Hill, revised by L. F. Powell, New York: Oxford University Press, 1934.

Justice Joseph Story's description of a corporation: Dartmouth College v. Woodward, 4 Wheat. 518 (1819).

The eighteenth-century classic case of corporate misgovernance: The Charitable Corporation v. Sir Robert Sutton, 2 ATK, 400 (1742).

The American Law Institute's discussion of personal liability: *Principles of Corporate Governance and Structure,* Tentative Draft No. 4, §4.01, Comment, American Law Institute, 1985.

"Gross non-attendance" in the *Francis* case and liability for the losses from the loans: Francis v. United Jersey Bank, 87 N.J. 15, 432 A.2d 814 (1981).

Texas Gulf Sulphur, the landmark insider case: SEC v. Texas Gulf Sulphur Company, 401 F.2d 833 (2d Cir. 1968).

Claims against directors for losses suffered in the management of a bank: Briggs v. Spaulding, 141 U.S. 132 (1891).

The best economic history of the American business corporation is A. Chandler, *The Visible Hand,* Cambridge: Harvard University Press, 1977.

CHAPTER 2.
Shark Repellents, Poison Pills, and Other Corporate Pharmacy

Chapter 2 is based on Moran v. Household International, Inc., 490 A.2d 1059 (Del. Ch.), affirmed, 500 A.2d 1346 (Del. 1985).

Value of takeovers and mergers in the 1980s: *New York Times*, June 21, 1987.

Donald Clark's background: Interview with Clark at Household International's headquarters, Prospect Heights, Illinois, July 15, 1987; Clark, testimony on direct examination.

Subsidiaries of Household International: Annual Report, 1984.

John Wilcox's analysis of the Household International shareholder profile, antitakeover proposals, and institutional investor reaction: Wilcox's testimony on direct examination.

Clark's comment on the lack of time to visit institutional investors and the dangers of calling a shareholders' meeting to adopt a fair-price amendment: Interview with Clark, July 15, 1987; Clark's testimony on direct examination.

Background on John Moran and DKM: The lower court case; "Executives Sign Up to Aid John Anderson," *Business Week*, July 7, 1980, 24; *Washington Post*, October 15, 1981.

How Moran was appointed to the board: Interview with Clark, July 15, 1987.

The purchase of Wallace-Murray: Interview with Clark, July 15, 1987; "A House Undivided," *Forbes*, September 9, 1985, 36, 40.

Moran's strategy of using certain of Household's assets to pay for the acquisition and his purchase of additional shares: *Forbes*, September 9, 1985, 36; Clark, testimony on direct examination.

Clark's reflections on Moran's deal and his strategy: Clark, testimony on direct examination; interview with Clark, July 15, 1987; *Forbes*, September 9, 1985, 36.

The unusual volume of activity in Household's stock in April and May 1984: Clark, testimony on direct examination.

Goldman, Sachs confirming the board's concern that Household was an undervalued situation: Clark, testimony on direct examination.

The grizzly bear scenario: Recorded at an American Law Institute–American Bar Association program, "Takeover Defenses and Directors' Liabilities," September 25–26, 1986, New York City.

Parts of the discussion of the poison pill: Arthur Fleischer, Jr., and Peter Golden, "Poison Pill," *National Law Journal*, February 24, 1986.

Clark referring to the board's flexibility to redeem the rights as a "string on the rights": Clark, testimony on direct examination; preview meeting of the board, August 13, 1984.

Martin Lipton and Peter Fahey's presentations at the August 14, 1984, board meeting: Minutes of the meeting of Household International's board of directors.

Moran's possible inclination to get involved in hostile takeovers: Interview with Clark, July 15, 1987.

Household's poison pill plan: From documents distributed to Household's directors and considered at the August 14, 1984, meeting of the board.

Household's statement regarding the impact of the rights: *Wall Street Journal,* August 20, 1984.

SEC reaction to Household's poison pill: "A Poison Pill That's Causing a Rash of Lawsuits," *Business Week,* April 1, 1985, 54.

February 15, 1985, board meeting and events thereafter: Interview with Clark, July 15, 1987.

Corporations that had adopted poison pills by mid-1987: *New York Times,* April 14, 1987. Clark's evaluation of Household's plan three years later: Interview with Clark, July 15, 1987.

"You can be a bull or a bear but you can't be a pig": Recorded at the American Law Institute–American Bar Association program "Takeover Defenses and Directors' Liabilities," September 25–26, 1986, New York City.

Money invested in mutual funds: *New York Times,* December 22, 1985. Antitakeover tactics of institutional investors: "The Battle for Corporate Control; Management Is Being Assailed from All Sides. Who's in Charge Here?" *Business Week,* May 18, 1987, 102.

CHAPTER 3.
Sauce for the Goose: The Exclusionary Self-tender

Chapter 3 is based on Unocal Corporation v. Mesa Petroleum Company, 493 A.2d 946 (Del. 1985).

Comments about and by Fred Hartley: *New York Times,* November 19, 1979, September 18, 1983, February 25, 1985, and April 16, 1985; *Los Angeles Times,* April 9, 1985; *Wall Street Journal,* May 24, 1985; deposition of Hartley, April 27, 1985.

Hartley on the possibility of merging Unocal into Mesa: *Los Angeles Times,* February 12, 1985; *Wall Street Journal,* May 24, 1985.

Federal response to hostile corporate takeovers: *New York Times,* April 3, 1985; *Los Angeles Times,* April 14, 1985. Testimony by New York City comptroller Harrison J. Goldin: House Subcommittee on Oversight, House Subcommittee on Select Revenue Measures, Public Hearings on Mergers and Acquisitions, Washington, D.C., April 1, 1985.

Hartley's reaction to Mesa's Schedule 13D filing and to greenmail: *Los Angeles Times,* April 25, 1985; *Washington Post,* April 7, 1985.

Goldman, Sachs retained in view of a possible proxy contest or other move by T. Boone Pickens: Deposition of Peter G. Sachs, May 3, 1985.

Pickens's plans for Unocal and Mesa's line of credit: *Los Angeles Times,* April 4, 1985, and May 22, 1985; *New York Times,* April 16, 1985; *Wall Street Journal,* May 24, 1985.

Hartley on the inadequacy of Mesa's offer and Unocal's April 13, 1985, board meeting to consider a defensive strategy: Deposition of Hartley, April 27, 1985; *Wall Street Journal,* May 24, 1985.

Unocal's board meeting of April 15, 1985, and the exchange offer: SEC filing, Unocal self-exchange offer, April 17, 1985; deposition of Hartley, April 27, 1985.

Analyst's comment on Unocal's restructuring: *New York Times,* April 16, 1985. .

Pickens's view of Unocal's defensive measures: "Is Unocal's 'Boone Bomb' More Than a Bluff?" *Business Week,* April 29, 1985, 29; *Los Angeles Times,* May 22, 23, and 24, 1985. Hartley's view: Deposition of Hartley; *Washington Post,* April 7, 1985; "Millions for Defense, Not One Cent for Tribute," *Forbes,* April 8, 1985, 40; *New York Times,* May 20, 1985.

The April 22, 1985, board meeting to review Mesa's exclusion from participating in the Unocal offer and amendment of the offer: SEC filing, supplement to exchange offer, April 24, 1985; deposition of Hartley, April 27, 1985.

Reverse greenmail: *Los Angeles Times,* May 22, 1985.

The costs of Unocal's independence: *New York Times,* December 22, 1986.

Hartley's attacks on corporate raiders and the status of Unocal: *Los Angeles Times,* May 13, 1985; *New York Times,* December 22, 1986.

CHAPTER 4.
Its Own White Knight

Chapter 4 is based on GAF Corporation v. Union Carbide Corporation, 624 F. Supp. 1016 (S.D.N.Y. 1985), and Gelco Corporation v. Coniston Partners, 652 F. Supp. 829 (D. Minn. October 10, 1986), affirmed, 811 F.2d 414 (8th Cir. 1987).

Bhopal: *New York Times,* December 8, 9, 10, 12, and 15, 1984; May 19, 1985.

Sam Heyman's evaluation of the effects of Bhopal on Union Carbide: "Restless GAF Is on the Prowl," *Fortune,* February 3, 1986, 32.

Sam Heyman's proxy campaign for GAF and GAF's turnaround: *Wall Street Journal,* December 12 and 14, 1983; *New York Times,* December 14, 1983, December 18, 1985; "Who's Afraid of Sam Heyman?" *Barrons,* August 26, 1985, 11; "The Proxy Fighter Who Is Turning Around GAF," *Fortune,* February 4, 1985, 84; "Restless GAF," February 3, 1986, 32.

Union Carbide's chairman and CEO, Warren Anderson, and the company: "Union Carbide Chief Faces Expulsion from India" and "Facing Up to the Crisis," *Financial Times,* December 8, 1984, 1, 32; *New York Times,* May 19, 1985, December 26, 1985.

Union Carbide's board, defensive measures and restructuring: Agreed Findings of Fact; minutes of the board of directors, July 24, 1985; Anderson, testimony on direct examination at trial; *New York Times,* December 10, 1985; SEC filing, Union Carbide Corporation self-exchange offer, December 7, 1985; interview with Harry Gray, Farmington, Connecticut, July 30, 1987.

Heyman's investment position in Union Carbide: *Barrons,* August 26, 1985; 11; Agreed Findings of Fact; Union Carbide Corporation self-exchange offer, December 7, 1985; *Wall Street Journal,* January 13, 1986; *Fortune,*

February 3, 1986; Anderson's testimony on direct examination; interview with Gray, July 30, 1987; Gray, testimony on direct examination.

GAF's hostile partial tender offer: Gray, testimony on direct examination; *New York Times*, December 10, 1985; SEC filing, supplement to Union Carbide self-exchange offer, December 10, 1985; "Sam Heyman's Hopeful Script for Carbide," *Business Week*, December 23, 1985, 30; Anderson, testimony on direct examination; interview with Gray, July 30, 1987.

Union Carbide's response to GAF's offer: Gray, testimony on direct examination; Agreed Findings of Fact; Anderson, testimony on direct examination; *New York Times*, December 18, 1985; *Wall Street Journal*, January 13, 1986; "Restless GAF," *Fortune*, February 3, 1986, 32; "Carbide Saves Itself — But Was It Worth It?" *Business Week*, January 20, 1986, 26; interview with Gray, July 30, 1987.

GAF raises its offer to $74 per share in cash: *New York Times*, December 26, 1985; *Wall Street Journal*, January 13, 1986.

Heyman's withdrawal: *Wall Street Journal*, January 9, 1986.

Anderson's comments on Wall Street as a casino: "Carbide Saves Itself," *Business Week*, January 20, 1986, 26.

Restructuring of Union Carbide and speech delivered by Robert D. Kennedy, Anderson's successor: "What Purina Really Wanted from Carbide," *Business Week*, April 21, 1986, 23; Robert D. Kennedy, "Strategic Planning," Vital Speeches of the Day, August 1, 1987, vol. LIII, no. 20, City News Publishing Company, Mount Pleasant, S.C.

Bud Grossman and Gelco Corporation: "Gelco: Debt and Losses Prompt the Leasing Giant to Give Up Its Freewheeling Ways," *Business Week*, March 12, 1984, 58; *New York Times*, September 1, 1986; *Wall Street Journal*, September 26, 1986.

Gelco's self-tender: *Wall Street Journal*, October 15, 1986.

Coniston Partners: "A Bid to Break Up NL Industries," *Business Week*, April 7, 1986, 44; "The Trio That Humbled Allegis," *Fortune*, July 20, 1987, 52.

The rise in Gelco's shares: *New York Times*, September 26, 1986.

Gelco's median breakup value: Affidavit of Tull N. Gearreald, Jr., managing director of Merrill Lynch.

Coniston's stake in Gelco: Coniston Partners revised tender offer filing, October 7, 1986; *Wall Street Journal*, October 8, 1986.

Coniston's sweetened bid: *Wall Street Journal*, October 24 and 27, 1986.

Keith Gollust's comment to the *Wall Street Journal* on the inadequacy of Gelco's offer: *Wall Street Journal*, October 31, 1986.

Gelco's acceptance of 63 percent of the total number of shares tendered: *PR Newswire*, November 13, 1986.

Gelco restructures: *Wall Street Journal*, November 10, 1986, March 18, 1987.

The friendly deal with General Electric Credit Corporation: *Wall Street Journal*, October 5, 1987.

CHAPTER 5.
Leveling the Playing Field

Chapter 5 is based on MacAndrews & Forbes Holdings, Inc., v. Revlon, Inc., 501 A.2d 1239 (Del. Ch. 1985), affirmed, 506 A.2d 173 (Del. 1986).

The rise of Ronald Perelman: Pantry Pride, Inc., Prospectus, July 12, 1985; "It wasn't enough," *Wall Street Journal*, August 23, 1985; *New York Times*, August 28, 1985; *Miami Herald*, August 10, 1985; *New York Times*, November 11, 1985; "The Shy Stripper," *New York*, November 18, 1985, 38; "25 Executives to Watch," *Business Week*, April 18, 1986, 230; *New York Times*, November 18, 1986.

Charles Revson's Revlon: "Businessmen in the News," *Fortune*, August 1974, 94; "Revlon After Revson," *Forbes*, September 15, 1975, 26; Andrew Tobias, *Fire and Ice*, New York: Warner Books, 1975.

Michel Bergerac: *New York Times*, July 18, 1974; "Revlon Grooms a New President," *Business Week*, July 27, 1974, 22; "Businessmen in the News," *Fortune*, August 1974, 94; "Management Realists in the Glamour World of Cosmetics," *Business Week*, November 29, 1976, 42; "Revlon After Revson," *Forbes*, September 15, 1975, 26. *New York Times*, August 22, 1985; November 6 and 11, 1985.

Initial meetings between Perelman and Bergerac: Minutes of Revlon's board of directors, August 19, 1985; Amended Complaint, October 14, 1985; *Wall Street Journal*, August 20, 1985.

Simon H. Rifkind: "Profiles," *New Yorker*, May 23, 1983, 46; affidavit of Simon H. Rifkind, October 16, 1985.

Revlon directors: "Revlon After Revson," *Forbes*, September 15, 1975, 26; Rifkind affidavit.

Board meeting of August 19, 1985, and the rights plan: Minutes of the board meeting; Rifkind affidavit; rights agreement, dated as of August 19, 1985, and summary of note purchase rights plan; *New York Times*, August 20, 1985.

Bergerac's position on offers to buy Revlon: *Wall Street Journal*, August 20, 1985.

Perelman's reaction to Revlon's rights plan and Pantry Pride's cash tender offer: *Wall Street Journal*, August 20, 1985; minutes of Revlon's board of directors, August 26, 1985; *Wall Street Journal*, August 23, 1986.

Meeting of Revlon's board of directors, August 26, 1985, and Revlon's exchange offer: SEC filing, Revlon, Inc., self-exchange offer, August 29, 1985, with letter to stockholders; minutes of the board, October 16, 1985; *New York Times*, August 27, 1985; Rifkind affidavit.

Pantry Pride's reduced bid: *Wall Street Journal*, September 16 and 30, 1985; minutes of Revlon's board of directors, September 24, 1985.

Letter dated September 27, 1985, from Perelman to Bergerac: Affidavit of Perelman, October 17, 1985, Exhibit A.

Perelman's increased offer of October 1, 1985: SEC filing, Amendment No. 4 to Revlon, Inc., Schedule 14D-9, September 24, 1985; Rifkind affidavit.

Revlon's deals with Forstmann Little and Adler & Shaykin: Amendment No. 4 to Revlon, Inc., Schedule 14D-9, September 24, 1985, including as exhibits the merger agreement and the asset sale agreement; minutes of Revlon's board of directors, October 3, 1985; *Wall Street Journal*, October 4, 1985; June 17, 1986; *New York Times*, October 14, 1985; Rifkind affidavit.

Lockups: Stephen Fraidin and Joseph Franco, "Lock-up Arrangements," 14 *Review of Securities Regulation*, 821 (Nov. 1981); Charles M. Nathan, "Lock-Ups and Leg-Ups: The Search for Security in the Acquisitions Market Place," Arthur Fleischer, Jr., chairman; Martin Lipton, Robert H. Mundheim, co-chairmen, Thirteenth Annual Institute on Securities Regulation, New York: Practicing Law Institute, 1981.

Revlon's irate noteholders: Rifkind affidavit.

Bergerac's withdrawal from the LBO: *New York Times*, October 14 and 15, 1985; Rifkind affidavit; "Bergerac Bows Out of the Revlon Deal," *Business Week*, October 28, 1985, 42.

Meeting of Revlon's board of directors, October 12, 1985: Minutes of the board; Rifkind affidavit.

Perelman's amended complaint: Amended Complaint, October 14, 1985; *New York Times*, October 19, 1985.

Revlon accepts Pantry Pride's offer of $58 per share: *New York Times*, November 4, 5, and 6, 1985; Adler & Shaykin's dispute with Perelman: *New York Times*, November 4, 1985, December 3, 1986; Revlon restructures: "Ron Perelman; Revlon's Striving Makeover Man," *Fortune*, January 5, 1987, 54.

Perelman takes Revlon private: "This Takeover Artist Wants to Be a Makeover Artist, Too," *Business Week*, December 1, 1986, 106; *New York Times*, March 7, 1987; "Perelman Buys Rest of Revlon," *Financial Times*, April 14, 1987, 34; "Perelman in Dollars 850M Buyout of Revlon Share-holders," *Financial Times*, April 15, 1987, 30; "Revlon's Chairman Takes the Company," *Business Week*, April 27, 1987, 43; "A Tale of Our Times," *Forbes*, May 18, 1987, 180; *New York Times*, January 1, 1988.

"A level playing field": American Law Institute–American Bar Association program, "Takeover Defenses and Directors' Liabilities," September 25–26, New York City.

CHAPTER 6.
On the Block: Management Buyouts and Open Bidding

Chapter 6 is based on Hanson Trust PLC v. ML SCM Acquisition, Inc., 781 F.2d 264 (2nd Cir. 1986) and Edelman v. Fruehauf Corporation, 798 F.2d 882 (6th Cir., 1986).

Hanson Trust's tender offer for SCM: "Restructured SCM 'Will Not Give Up Without a Fight' " and "Hanson: Bigger Yet and Bigger; The Bid for SCM," *Financial Times*, August 23, 1985, 10; *New York Times*, August 23,

1985; offer to purchase for cash any and all outstanding shares of common stock of SCM Corporation, August 26, 1985.

Backgrounds of Lord Hanson and Sir Gordon White: "Much More Than a Predator; Profile of Lord Hanson," *Financial Times,* December 23, 1983, 6; "Back to Basics at Hanson," *Financial Times,* August 23, 1985, 12; "The Managers," *Dun's Business Month,* October 1985, 7; "Toughest Test for the Expatriate Englishman; Hanson's Battle for SCM," *Financial Times,* October 5, 1985, 7; "Hanson Trust's U.S. Thrust," *Fortune,* October 14, 1985, 47; "Hanson's Track Record Wins the Day," *Financial Times,* April 12, 1986, 4; "Reshuffling of Assets," *Financial Times,* September 19, 1986, 24.

SCM Corporation and the company's strategy: "Restructured SCM 'Will Not Give Up Without a Fight,'" *Financial Times,* August 23, 1985, 10; Paul Elicker, testimony on direct examination; SCM Corporation self-exchange offer, October 18, 1985.

Hanson Trust's moves through Rothschild, Inc., and Skadden, Arps: SCM Corporation self-exchange offer, October 18, 1985.

Elicker's views on Wall Street "players": "Back to Basics at Hanson," *Financial Times,* August 23, 1985, 10.

Cross-examination of Kenneth Miller on the financing of SCM's offer and other issues: Miller, transcript of trial testimony.

Merrill Lynch's protective measures: Elicker, transcript of trial testimony.

SCM conference-call board meeting of August 30, 1985, re Merrill Lynch LBO: SEC filing, SCM Corporation self-exchange offer, October 18, 1985.

Hanson's reaction to SCM–Merrill Lynch LBO: Elicker, transcript of trial testimony.

Letter from White to Elicker, September 10, 1985: SCM Corporation self-exchange offer, October 18, 1985.

SCM's board meeting, September 10, 1985, discussing Merrill Lynch offer at $74 and the lockup: Miller, transcript of trial testimony; affidavit of Willard J. Overlock, Jr.; Elicker, transcript of trial testimony.

Hanson withdrawal of $72 offer and the company's purchase of additional shares: Miller, transcript of trial testimony; *New York Times,* October 5, 1986; SCM Corporation self-exchange offer, October 18, 1985.

SCM board meeting, October 10, 1985, and the rejection of Hanson's new offer: SCM Corporation self-exchange offer, October 18, 1985.

Hanson proceeds with its $75 per share offer: *New York Times,* January 7, 1986; *Wall Street Journal,* January 8 and 9, 1986; "A Master's Touch in Buying and Selling Companies," *Financial Times,* September 19, 1986, 8.

The ventures of Asher Edelman: "Newest Kid on the Takeover Block: Boone, Carl, Vic — Make Room for Asher Edelman," *Barrons,* March 11, 1985, 8; "Fruehauf Tries to Dodge Asher Edelman," *Business Week,* June 30, 1986, 38.

Fruehauf Corporation: Annual Report, 1985; *New York Times,* March 25, 1987.

Edelman's acquisition of Fruehauf shares in the open market, his attempt to meet with Fruehauf chairman, Robert Rowan, and Edelman's proposal for a cash merger, and cash tender at $44 per share: *New York Times,* March 25, 1986, April 5, 1986, May 2, 1986; SEC filing, tender offer by Edelman Group for Fruehauf Corporation, June 13, 1986; "Fruehauf Tries to Dodge Edelman," *Business Week,* June 30, 1986, 38.

Business Week comment on Fruehauf's strategy: "Fruehauf Tries to Dodge Edelman," *Business Week,* June 30, 1986, 38. Edelman's profit: *New York Times,* August 23, 1986.

The New Princes of Industry

Allegis's firing of Richard J. Ferris and the company's recapitalization: *New York Times,* June 11, 12, and 21, 1987.

Bids for parts of Allegis: *New York Times,* June 11 and 22, 1987; *Wall Street Journal,* June 30, 1987.

Fred Hartley on the status of Unocal after Mesa's attack: *New York Times,* December 22, 1986.

GTE Corporation's charter provisions to allow boards to consider nonfinancial factors: SEC filing, GTE, notice of special meeting of shareholders, November 21, 1986.

o   o   o

Index

Commitment fees, 181, 185–186, 188
Compensation
    directors, 65
    management, 4–5, 65
Competition, 4, 5
    effects of, 52–53
Conflict of interest, 26, 108, 152, 177,
    186
    compensation and, 4–5, 65
    in leveraged buyout by management of
        Trans Union Corporation, 19
Congress
    hearings on hostile corporate take-
        overs, 96–97
    legislation concerning golden para-
        chutes, 65
Coniston Partners, 191, 192
    takeover attempt of Gelco Corporation,
        128–131
Coniston Partners, Gelco Corporation v.,
    129–131, 194, 195
Corporate assets, real value, 6
Corporate authority to deal in its own
    stock, 108
Corporate bonds. *See* Securities
Corporate competence, 11–12, 132. *See
    also* Business judgment rule; Liabil-
    ity
Corporate corruption, 11–12, 62–63. *See
    also* Business judgment rule; Liabil-
    ity
    in *Charitable Corporation v. Sir Robert
        Sutton,* 52–57
Corporate finance, changes in, 4
Corporate raiders, 78, 146. *See also* Take-
    overs
    Coniston Partners, 128–131, 191, 192
    Edelman, Asher, 178–183
    Hanson, Lord James Edward, 160–
        178
    Heyman, Samuel J., 112–125
    Perelman, Ronald Owen, 135, 136–
        137, 139–159
    Pickens, T. Boone, 91–111
    Pritzker, Jay A., 19–33, 37
    Unicorp Canada Corporation, 127
Corporate taxation, 4
Corporate-governance law, 11–12, 57,
    194. *See also* specific cases
    constitutive rule, 107–108
    corporate authority to deal in its own
        stock, 108
    process and, 37–39
Corporations
    advantages of, 45
    charter, 45, 51
        amendment of, 75

amending to allow consideration of
    nonfinancial factors, 198–199
control in, 7–8, 10–11, 95, 193. *See
    also* Takeovers; Tender offer
early historical roots, 43–48
as an entity independent of its individ-
    ual members, 45–46, 51
large, emergence of, 57
legal concept of, 51
misgovernance, in *Charitable Corpora-
    tion v. Sir Robert Sutton,* 52–57
owning other corporations, 49–51
structure, 46–47, 51, 57
Council of Institutional Investors, 88
Creedon, John J., 115
Creeping acquisition. *See* Toehold acqui-
    sition

D & O insurance. *See* Liability, insurance
Dartmouth College v. Woodward, 51–52
Datapoint Corporation, 179
de Tocqueville, Alexis, 12
Debt, 158
Debt securities. *See* Securities
Debt/equity ratio, 92
Delaware Corporation Law, Section
    141(a), 107–108
Delaware Corporation Law, Section
    160(a), 108
DeLorean, John, 138
Democracy in America, 12
Dillon, Read, 101
Diocese, as an early form of a corporation,
    45–46
Directors. *See also* Corporate-governance
    law; Corporations; Takeovers
    accountability, 86–87, 110, 195–196
    agency law and, 57–58
    authority regarding mergers and ac-
        quisitions, 193–194
    combination with the chief executive
        officer, 46–47
    compensation, 65
    concept of oversight by, 69
    considering nonfinancial factors in
        evaluating a takeover attempt, 198–
        199
    and control in corporations, 193
    criminal liability, 59
    distinction from management, 47, 68–
        69
    duties, 46, 47, 52–70. *See also* specific
        duties
    duty of care, 33–34, 62–63, 64, 67–
        70, 176–178
    duty of loyalty, 62, 64–66. *See also*
        Trust